Discover Hidden Nature Treasures in Florida

Sarah .B Mclean

Funny helpful tips:

Engage with the potential of zero-knowledge proofs; they enhance data privacy in transactions without revealing specifics.

Practice mutual patience; understanding takes time.

Discover Hidden Nature Treasures in Florida : Uncover Florida's Best-Kept Secret Nature Getaways: Your Guide to Off-The-Beaten-Path Adventures.

Life advices:

Prioritize emotional intimacy; it's the bedrock of a deep and lasting bond.

Rotate between different literary movements; from Romanticism to Modernism, each offers unique stylistic and thematic concerns.

Introduction

This is a comprehensive guide that provides birders and wildlife enthusiasts with valuable information about various clusters and locations along the birding and wildlife trail in Florida. The guide is organized into different clusters, each representing specific areas with unique bird and wildlife viewing opportunities.

The clusters featured in the guide include Myakka River, Sandpiper, Charlotte Harbor, Piping Plover, Wood Stork, Short-tailed Hawk, Okeechobee, Spoonbill, Mangrove, Cypress, Snail Kite, Whistling-Duck, Night-Heron, Cuckoo, Pine Rockland, White-Crowned Pigeon, and Key West and Tortugas.

Each cluster is described in detail, providing birdwatchers and wildlife viewers with essential information about the locations, species of birds and wildlife commonly found in those areas, and any specific features or highlights that make each cluster unique.

The guide also includes sections on how to contribute to maintaining the trail, identifying birds and wildlife, and providing feedback on the trail experience. It emphasizes the importance of ethical birding and wildlife viewing practices, as well as additional resources and information for birdwatchers and wildlife enthusiasts.

For those interested in the Wings Over Florida Program, the guide provides relevant information and highlights how birders and wildlife viewers can support conservation efforts through their activities.

To aid readers in using the guide effectively, a map key is included, which likely provides explanations of various symbols, icons, and colors used on the trail map.

Overall, this book serves as a valuable resource for birdwatchers and wildlife enthusiasts, offering a wealth of information to enhance their experiences along the trail and contribute to the conservation of Florida's diverse bird and wildlife populations.

Contents

Map A
Myakka River
Cluster

▌Quick Point Nature
▌Preserve

This site is an interesting mix of mangrove estuary, tidal swamps and uplands, all being restored to natural function. Walking from the parking area at Overlook Park, you pass under a bridge and onto a short trail system that leads along stretches of Sarasota Bay. This conjunction makes the site not only fruitful for waders such as herons and egrets, ibises and spoonbills, but also "flyovers" like ospreys, gulls and terns from the beach side. Check the boardwalk overlooks at low tide for shorebirds and peeps, and stop by during spring migration season to look for warblers and flycatchers in the canopy.

Directions: From intersection of US 41 and SR 780 (Fruitville Rd.) in Sarasota, drive 0.2 mi. south on US 41, and turn right onto SR 789/John Ringling Blvd. Continue west across causeway for 3.6 mi., turning right (N) to stay on SR 789 through Harding ("St. Armand's) Circle, to the preserve parking area at Overlook Park, the first left after crossing New Pass Bridge onto Longboat Key. Enter the walkway under bridge to access the preserve.

Open all year, 5 a.m. to dusk. (941) 316-1988
www.longboatkey.org/parks/quick_point.htm

2 Arlington Park

This small site is worth stopping by quickly to check a few specific areas. Offering patches of hardwood hammock, a 1.5-acre lake, and a small reclaimed swamp within one of the most densely developed parts of the city, there is no telling what may stop in here briefly or might even decide to nest. The 0.7-mile paved walkway through this urban park provides a low-stress option to other more strenuous sites. You will find common moorhens and occasionally a purple gallinule in the swamp, along with smaller waders such as little blue herons and snowy egrets. The hardwoods harbor warblers and vireos, and the occasional thrush will sing during the spring. Check the lake for wood ducks as well as other migratory species.

Directions: From intersection of US 41 and Bahia Vista St. in Sarasota, drive 0.9 mi. east on Bahia Vista, turn right (S) on Tuttle Ave., continue 0.3 mi. and turn right (W) on Waldemere St. The entrance is 0.1 mi. on the left.

Open all year, dawn to dusk. (941) 861-5000 www.scgov.net

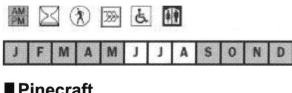

3 Pinecraft Park

This small 15-acre site contains a mesic hammock habitat located at the south end of the park that is unique in south Florida. Its character feels much more northern with its high, dense canopy of elms, hickories and oaks. Visit during early spring and look and listen for thrushes, wrens, warblers, vireos, flycatchers – just about any small migratory species passing through will make a stopover in this oasis. Check the overlooks along the edges of Phillipi Creek, where resident species such as herons, moorhens and ibises share the water with waterthrushes and common yellowthroats. Sharp-shinned and Cooper's hawks will find the canopy appealing, both for resting and for hunting. Wood ducks are not uncommon in this unusual mix of wood and water.

Directions: From intersection of US 41 and Bahia Vista St. in Sarasota, drive 1.5 mi. east on Bahia Vista, turn right (S) on Carter Ave., continue 0.1 mi. and turn right on Gilbert Ave. The park is 0.1 mi. at the end of the road.

Open all year, dawn to dusk. (941) 861-5000 www.scgov.net

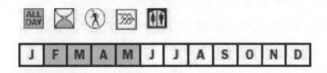

Celery Fields

This county-owned flood mitigation area was built in the 1990s on a former agricultural site, and it has proven to be one of the premier birding hotspots on the southwest coast with 206 species seen. An open landscape offers long-range vistas of flooded fields, freshwater marsh and open water. As a result, birders scoping from the gazebo or walking the berm trail system around the retention ponds can spot waders such as herons and egrets, ducks and grebes on the water, and everything from sparrows to harriers over the grassy fields. Some notable species include sandhill crane, limpkin, mottled duck, black-bellied whistling duck, bobolink and bald eagle. This area continues to undergo great changes, but don't be discouraged by the development when you visit. The birds have found this protected area and are thriving, with more species showing up as more of this habitat is restored to the natural sawgrass wetland it was 100 years ago.

Directions: From I-75 exit 210 (SR 780, Fruitville Rd.), drive 0.5 mi. east on SR 780, turn right (S) on Coburn Rd., continue 1.0 mi. to Palmer Blvd. and turn left (E); parking area is 0.5 mi. on left at gazebo.

Open all year, dawn to dusk. (941) 861-5000 www.scgov.net

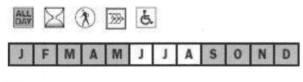

5 Crowley Museum and Nature Center

This site contains more than 2 miles of trails through five native habitats (pine flatwoods, hardwood hammocks, freshwater marsh and swamp, and riverine areas) and includes a 2000-foot boardwalk terminating at an observation tower overlooking the marsh. Species that call this site home include red-shouldered hawks and great crested flycatchers, white-eyed vireos and northern parulas. Bald eagles and barred owls nest here, swallow-tailed kites cruise through during summer and dabbling ducks visit the swamps and marsh during winter. This site has records for black-bellied whistling-duck, crested caracara and even vermillion flycatcher! Call ahead to find out the schedules for the Saturday workshop series and other educational programs that occur throughout the year.

Directions: From I-75 exit 210 (SR 780, Fruitville Rd.), drive 11.0 mi. east on SR 780 and turn right (S) on Myakka Rd. (CR 780). The entrance is 2.4 mi. on the left (E).

Open 10 a.m.to 4 p.m., (941) 322-1000 www.cmncfl.org

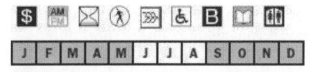

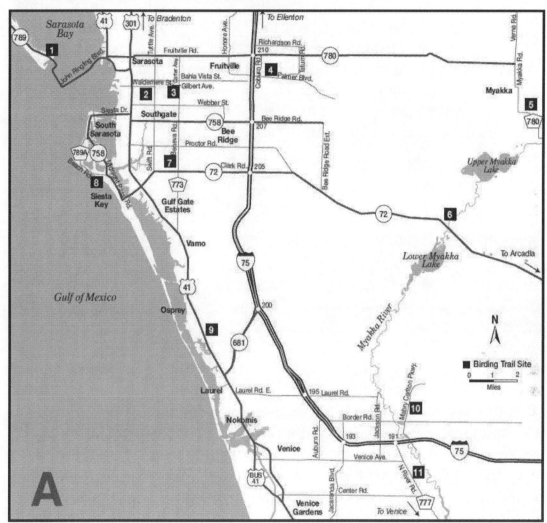

Myakka River State Park

This is one of the largest of Florida's state parks, and it will easily keep you birding and exploring all day long. Take the 7-mile scenic drive through shady hammocks and grassy marshes and along the Upper Myakka lakeshore. From Oct.-Apr., ducks, wading birds, shorebirds, ospreys and eagles are seen from the lakeshore, the Birdwalk, or by canoeing along the river's grassy edges. Don't miss the elevated canopy walkway through an oak-palm hammock and the 74-foot-high observation tower. Explore pine flatwoods, hammocks, seasonal wetlands and globally imperiled Florida dry prairie via a 39-mile hiking trail. You'll find exhibits and movies in the Visitor Center. Stop at the Ranger Station for trail maps and park information. Park may close when flooded; check web for updates.

Directions: From I-75 exit 205 (SR 72, Clark Rd.), drive 9 mi. east on SR 72 to the entrance on the left (N).

Open all year, 8 a.m. to sunset. (941) 361-6511
www.floridastateparks.org/myakkariver

7 Red Bug Slough Preserve

This site, part of the county's environmental lands program, contains beautiful mesic hammock habitat that is just waiting for birders to document what lives there. Already known for fallouts of warblers during migration, this property also provides habitat for species such as belted kingfishers, green herons, limpkins, wood ducks and mottled ducks. Least terns are a surprising visitor to the slough. The short, developed trail system at the main parcel is easy walking through the hammock and along the slough; the more adventurous may want to look into the adjoining, undeveloped parcel to the northwest that contains denser understory.

Directions: From the intersection of US 41 and SR 72 (Stickney Point Rd.) in south Sarasota, drive 1.8 mi. east on SR 72 (becomes Clark Rd.) and turn left (N) on Beneva Rd. The entrance is 0.5 mi. on the left (W).

Open all year, 7:30 a.m. to 8 p.m. (Daylight Savings Time); 7:30 a.m. to 6 p.m. (winter). (941) 861-5000 www.scgov.net

8 Siesta Beach

Listed among the top 10 beaches in the world (for humans), this site is best birded early in the morning or later in the evening when it is quiet and less crowded. Walk 1.5 miles in either direction from the parking area, sharing the white sand with willets, dunlins and ruddy turnstones. Overhead, watch for least terns (among others) as they dive the surf with the pelicans and ospreys. Snowy egrets are sometimes found exploring the wrackline, with hosts of gulls waiting to snatch any worthwhile treasures.

Directions: From the intersection of US 41 and SR 72 (Stickney Point Rd.) in south Sarasota, drive 1.0 mi. west on SR 72, turn right (N) on SR 758 (Midnight Pass Rd.) and drive 1.2 mi. to the road fork. At this fork, bear left onto CR 789A (Beach Rd.). The entrance is 0.3 mi. on the left (W).

Open all year, 6 AM to midnight. (941) 861-5000 www.scgov.net

9 Oscar Scherer State

▌Park

More than 12 miles of hiking and biking trails within this park will introduce you to large areas of scrubby flatwoods, home to one of the densest populations of Florida scrub-jays in southwest Florida. This habitat, which is closely managed for these birds' benefit, gives way at times to cooler walks beside South Creek, through the campground, and around Lake Osprey – all great places to be during migration as the warblers and vireos settle into the canopy to feed in this oasis. The scrub-jays share this park with nesting bald eagles, and sandhill cranes even raise their young in the northernmost part of the park. Call ahead for scheduled walks or to organize group trips.

Directions: From intersection of US 41 and US 41 Business Route (Tamiami Trail) north of Venice, drive appx. 4.4 mi. north on US 41 to park entrance on right (E). Or, from I-75 southbound, take exit 200 and follow SR 681 south to US 41, then turn right (N) on US 41. From I-75 northbound, take exit 195 and follow Laurel Rd. west to US 41, then turn right (N) on US 41 as above.

Open all year, 8 a.m. to sundown. (941) 483-5956
www.floridastateparks.org/oscarscherer

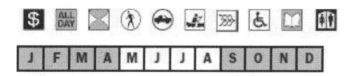

▌1 T. Mabry Carlton, Jr. Memorial
0 Reserve

Depending on the scale of the experience you are looking for, this site offers a little bit of everything. The main public use area is a little more than 100 acres and offers trails through hardwood hammock and pine flatwoods (listen for Bachman's sparrows), and around freshwater marsh and forested swamp (hotspots for migrating warblers). For the more adventurous, the full 24,500 acres of the preserve borders the huge Myakka River State Park and offer continuous trails and power line rights-of-way that can be hiked or biked as far as you care to go. Include prairie and oak scrub to the list of habitat types already mentioned and you have an idea of the diversity that awaits you. Call ahead for trail conditions and to request a backcountry map. Be sure to take plenty of water and sunscreen. Park may close when flooded.

Directions: From I-75 exit 193 (Jacaranda Blvd.), drive north 0.7 mi., turn right (E) on Border Rd., continue 2.5 mi. and turn left on Mabry Carlton Pkwy.; entrance is 0.3 mi. on right.

Open all year, 7:30 a.m. to 8 p.m. (Daylight Savings Time); 7:30 a.m. to 6 p.m. (winter). (941) 861-5000 www.scgov.net

11 Jelks Preserve

This 600-acre site consists of pine flatwoods and mesic hammocks with remnant wet prairie and freshwater swamp, all bordered by the hardwood-lined Myakka River. These sandy trails will take you through warbler and vireo habitat, under canopies of bromeliad-fringed hardwoods that are home to pileated woodpeckers and barred owls. At the river overlooks you will find ospreys and white ibises, egrets and herons, and sometimes wood storks. Take plenty of water and be sure to get a trail map from the kiosk, then explore the less-shaded scrub trails looking for eastern towhees and eastern bluebirds.

Directions: From I-75 exit 191 (CR 777, N. River Rd.), drive 1.5 mi. south on CR 777 to the entrance on the left (E).

Open all year, 7:30 a.m. to 8 p.m. (Daylight Savings Time); 7:30 a.m. to 6 p.m. (winter). (941) 861-5000 www.scgov.net

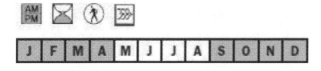

Map B
Sandpiper
Cluster

1 Venice Area Audubon
2 Rookery

An easily-accessible roosting and resting area for a variety of wading birds, this site is great for those who like to sit still and watch closely. Offering a covered pavilion for shade and plenty of pond-side grassy areas for lawn chairs, this small site has become a mecca for bird photography. Less than a stone's throw from the shoreline, herons, egrets, anhingas and ibises pose and repose, seemingly unconcerned by the people watching them. Come during late spring and early summer and watch as parents delicately feed and brood their ungainly offspring – truly a special glimpse into these birds' lives. Scan the pond edges for common moorhens, purple gallinules and smaller birds such as yellowthroats. Birds are forming a second rookery in the recently-acquired wetlands across the road. Check out the Audubon Visitor Center located 0.1 miles north of the parking area (west side) for recent sightings.

Directions: From intersection of US 41 and SR 776 (Englewood Rd.) in Venice, drive 0.4 mi. south on US 41 and turn right (S) on Annex Rd; parking area at shelter is 0.2 mi. ahead on the left.

Open all year, dawn to dusk. (941) 496-8984 www.veniceaudubon.org

J	F	M	A	M	J	J	A	S	O	N	D

13 Shamrock Park and Nature Center

This park, which is a trail connector to the Venetian Waterways Trail and Caspersen Beach (site #14), contains coastal scrub which the county works hard to maintain. As a result, this is one of the best sites in the area to spot Florida scrub-jays. The two closely monitored families of jays here (along with neighboring Caspersen Beach) are as likely to be seen along the ADA-accessible paved walkway as they are on the scrub trail system. The local Audubon chapter census for this park documented 118 bird species, but for scrub-jays, this one's a sure bet.

Directions: From intersection of US 41 and US 41 Business Route south of Venice, drive 0.1 mi. south and turn right (W) on Shamrock Dr. The park entrance is 1.7 mi. on the right.

Open all year, dawn to dusk; Visitor Center open 8 a.m. to 4 p.m., Mon.-Fri. (941) 861-5000 www.scgov.net

J	F	M	A	M	J	J	A	S	O	N	D

14 Caspersen Beach

This county park boasts 2 miles of Gulf coast beach, replete with all the gulls, terns and shorebirds one might expect. Walk the beach or through the coastal hammock, which offers sanctuary for warblers during migration. Canoe or kayak into Red Lake and skim the mangrove edges for close-up views of waders such as reddish egrets and night-herons during high tide, or scan the mudflats from the boat ramp at low tide for more shorebirds. One of the biggest draws of this site, along with neighboring Shamrock Park, is an island of remnant scrub habitat that hosts two families of Florida scrub-jays; slowly walk the trails and watch and listen carefully.

Directions: From intersection of US 41 and Venice Ave. in Venice, drive appx. 1 mi. west on Venice Ave. and turn left (S) on Harbor Dr. S. The park is appx. 3 mi. ahead at the end of the road.

Open all year, 6 a.m. to midnight. (941) 861-5000 www.scgov.net

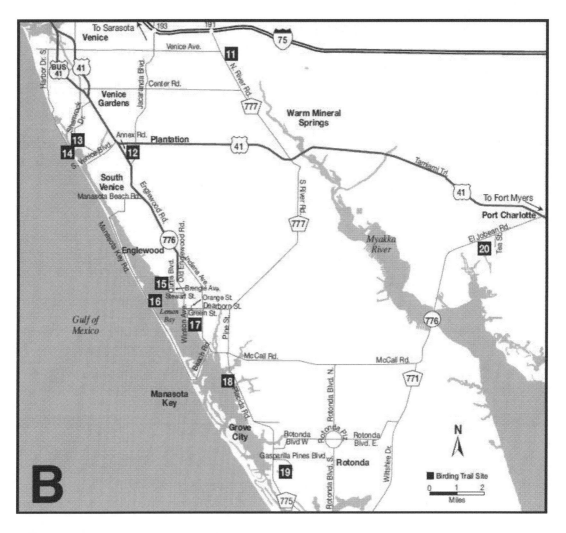

1 5 Lemon Bay Park and Environmental Center

Situated on the shore of Lemon Bay Aquatic Preserve, this park offers a mile of coastal trail as well as 2.2 miles of trails into pine flatwoods. Scan the beach from overlooks along the Bayside Trail (0.5 mile) for shorebirds such as least and western sandpipers. Watch the open water during winter months for common loons and red-breasted mergansers. Five different tern species have been recorded here, and magnificent frigatebirds sometimes occur. Migration brings hungry warblers and vireos to the wax myrtles, and the shallows host swifts and swallows. Trails through the flatwoods will provide views of red-shouldered hawks, breeding pine warblers and several different woodpeckers. Be sure to ask about nesting bald eagles, and keep an eye out for wood ducks, which have also nested on the property.

Directions: From I-75 exit 191 (CR 777, N. River Rd.), go south on CR 777. Cross US 41 (where S. River Rd. begins) and continue several miles; S. River Rd. will become Dearborn St. Stay on Dearborn into Englewood. Cross SR 776 (Indiana Ave.), then turn right onto Old Englewood Rd. Turn left onto Stewart St. Turn right onto Curtis Blvd. Turn left on Brengle Ave. The park is at the end of the street.

Open all year, dawn to dusk; environmental center is open Mon.-Fri., 9 a.m. to 3 p.m.; Sat.-Sun., 9 a.m. to 2 p.m.
(941) 861-5000
www.scgov.net

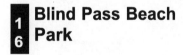

16 Blind Pass Beach Park

Encompassing a mile of relatively unvisited Gulf shore, this is the perfect site in this county for uninterrupted beach birding. More common shoreline species are ubiquitous: spotted sandpiper, willet, dunlin and black-bellied plover. Across the street is a short trail through mangrove swamp that leads to a lagoon off of Lemon Bay Aquatic Preserve. Scan the mudflats at low tide for more shorebirds and watch the mangrove edges for wading birds, including reddish egret. Launch a canoe or kayak from the small ramp and spend some time floating the lagoon and bay.

Directions: From intersection of US 41 and SR 776 (Englewood Rd.) in Venice, drive 2.0 mi. south on SR 776, turn right (W) on Manasota Beach Rd., continue 1.7 mi. (cross over Lemon Bay) and turn left (S) on Manasota Key Rd.; entrance is 3.7 mi. on left.

Open all year, 6 a.m. to midnight. (941) 861-5000
www.scgov.net

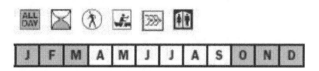

17 Indian Mound Park

Almost a true "postage stamp" park, this tiny site offers a place for either a quick scan of the bay or a comfortable spot to set up a scope for an hour while you have lunch. Only 7 acres in size, this site provides a vista over Lemon Bay, where you can see American oystercatchers, ruddy turnstones and western sandpipers, as well as a host of other shorebirds at low tide. Osprey and bald eagles hunt the bay, and terns and gulls carve the air overhead. While here, take a stroll along the wooded trail over the prehistoric Indian Mound; look and listen for migratory species as you walk. Come during winter for views of common loons and red-breasted mergansers.

Directions: From intersection of SR 776 (McCall Rd.) and Dearborn St. in Englewood, turn left (W) on Dearborn St. After appx. 0.5 mi., turn left on Orange St., right on Green St., and left again on Winson Ave., all in rapid succession. The park is at end of Winson Ave.

Open all year, 6 a.m. to midnight. (941) 861-5000
www.scgov.net

18 CHEC Cedar Point Environmental Park

Situated on a small protected peninsula that juts into Lemon Bay Aquatic Preserve, this site offers a green haven within the rapidly developing communities around Englewood. A trail system through flatwoods and coastal marsh will lead you past everything from white and glossy ibises to great horned owls and down to the bay, where you will find common loons and bay ducks in winter and a variety of herons and egrets all year long. Nesting bald eagles require some trail closures during spring and early summer, but there is still plenty to see.

Directions: From intersection of SR 776 (McCall Rd.) and CR 775 (Placida Rd.) south of Englewood, drive 1.0 mi. south on CR 775 to the entrance on the right (W).

Open all year, sunrise to sunset; educational center open Mon.-Fri., 8:30 a.m. to 4:30 p.m. (941) 475-0769
www.checflorida.org, www.charlottecountyfl.com

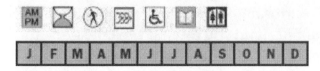

19 Amberjack Environmental Park

This 220-acre preserve offers trail loops through scrubby oak and pine flatwoods, with an open water marsh providing variety. Here you can find many of the species associated with the scrub and flatwood community: woodpeckers, resident warblers such as pine, palm, and yellow-rumped, and many gnatcatchers and towhees. The central wetland area offers wading birds, both pelicans, both teal, and a collection of other water-associated birds such as red-winged blackbird, common yellowthroat and eastern phoebe. Least sandpipers have also been found at the wetland, and the northern loop trail is home to a family of Florida scrub-jays, so look closely!

Directions: From intersection of SR 776 (McCall Rd.) and CR 775 (Placida Rd.) south of Englewood, drive 4.6 mi. south on CR 775 and turn left (E) on Gasparilla Pines Blvd. The entrance is 1.1 mi. at the end of the road.

Open all year, dawn to dusk. (941) 764-4360
www.charlottecountyfl.com

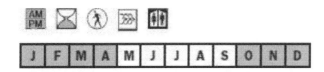

Tippecanoe Environmental Park
20

Don't let the Minor League quality sports park fool you; this 350-acre preserve offers a variety of habitats including flatwoods, scrub, mangroves and tidal creeks, all surrounding a large central lake. Trail systems starting behind the ballfields lead you around the lake (look for mottled ducks, common moorhens and the occasional king rail), then into well-maintained scrub and flatwoods where pine and prairie warblers are neighbors to an established family of Florida scrub-jays. The entrance at the end of Tea St. will take you along a tidal creek past black-necked stilts and white and glossy ibises to "Mount Tippecanoe," a spoil pile with a commanding view of the entire site.

Directions: From intersection of US 41 and SR 776 (El Jobean Rd./Veterans Blvd./McCall Rd.) in Port Charlotte, drive 2.4 mi. west on

SR 776 to the main entrance on the left (look for the baseball park). Tea St. access is 0.6 mi. east on SR 776. The entrance gate is at the dead-end of this short road.

Open all year, dawn to dusk. (941) 764-4360
www.charlottecountyfl.com

Map C
Charlotte Harbor
Cluster

2 **1** Charlotte Harbor Environmental Center: Alligator Creek Preserve

This small site is actually part of a much larger aquatic buffer preserve. Three loop trails offer almost 5 miles of possibilities, not including a longer spur trail into the buffer preserve itself. They will take you through very different habitat types: one through pine flatwoods that harbor red-shouldered hawks and downy and red-bellied woodpeckers, and the other around freshwater marsh and through remnant tropical hammock where you will see wrens and vireos. You may hear or actually catch sight of an eastern screech-owl. Walk carefully and be aware that there is a lot of poison ivy here.

Directions: From intersection of US 41, SR 768 (Jones Loop Rd.), and CR 765 (Burnt Store Rd.) south of Punta Gorda, drive 1.2 mi. south on CR 765 to the entrance on the right (W).

Open all year, dawn to dusk; visitor center open Mon.-Sat., 9 a.m. to 3 p.m.; Sun., 11 a.m. to 3 p.m. (941) 575-5435
www.checflorida.org

2 **2** 22 Charlotte Harbor Preserve State Park: Old Datsun Trail

20

In addition to two isolated wetlands, this site offers pine flatwoods mixed with oak/cabbage palm hammocks in an interesting example of habitat succession from agricultural fields to wild lands. A 1.75-mile loop trail gives you the chance to find white-eyed vireos, screech-owls and great horned owls, and red-shouldered hawks in the uplands. Be sure to walk the well-marked spur trails to the wetlands for views of green herons, wood storks and white and glossy ibises. Watch for the occasional swallow-tailed kite overhead. A visit at dusk may yield views of chuck-will's-widows.

Directions: From intersection of US 41, SR 768 (Jones Loop Rd.), and CR 765 (Burnt Store Rd.) south of Punta Gorda, drive 2.7 mi. south on CR 765 to the trailhead parking on the right (W).

Open all year, dawn to dusk. (941) 575-5861
www.floridastateparks.org/charlotteharbor

2 Fred C. Babcock/Cecil M. Webb Wildlife Management
3 Area

With more than 65,000 acres of the finest intermixed pine flatwoods and freshwater marsh in the state (sprinkled with hardwood hammocks and dry prairie), this Wildlife Management Area (WMA) will keep you busy all day long. Drive or bike the roads (4WD not necessary), walk the trails, or take your canoe out onto Webb Lake. Two of the biggest draws for this property are singing Bachman's sparrows in the spring and easily-accessed red-cockaded woodpecker colonies (ask for a map at the WMA headquarters; office open 8 a.m. to 5 p.m. Mon.-Fri.). Some of the other highlights for this property include American and least bitterns, king rail, sandhill crane, wild turkey, sedge wren, brown-headed nuthatch and many, many more. Check website for hunt dates.

Directions: Entrance to the WMA is immediately east of I-75 at exit 158 (Tucker Grade).

Open all year, sunrise to sunset. (863) 648-3200
MyFWC.com/viewing/recreation/wmas/lead/fred-babcockwebb

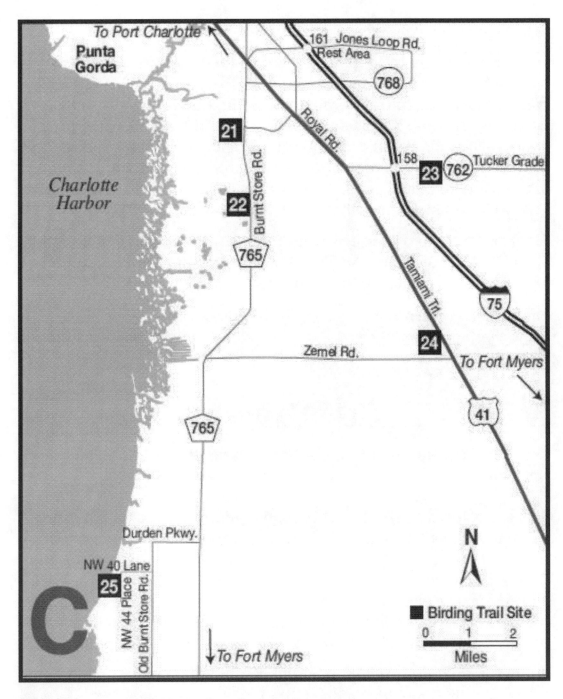

Charlotte Flatwoods Environmental Park

Adjacent to the much larger Babcock/Webb WMA, this site is also dominated by pine flatwoods and can offer a similar experience on a much smaller scale. Trails around the perimeter through the flatwoods offer sparrows and warblers, vireos and flycatchers. Follow the main trail straight in from the gate and you will find yourself on a raised spoil pile overlooking a flooded borrow pit, a surprisingly pleasant feature which contains belted kingfishers, waders such as wood stork and white ibis, and a small community of dabbling ducks during winter.

Directions: From intersection of US 41, SR 768 (Jones Loop Rd.), and CR 765 (Burnt Store Rd.) south of Punta Gorda, drive 7.4 mi. south on US 41 to the entrance on the right (W).

Open all year, dawn to dusk. (941) 764-4360
www.charlottecountyfl.com

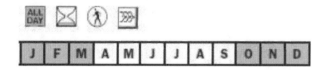

25 Charlotte Harbor Preserve State Park: North Cape Flats Trail

This site offers a 1.0-mile trail through predominately pine flatwoods that ends at Charlotte Harbor, where coastal berm and mudflats provide an end-of-hike treat. Plan your walk so that you arrive at low tide. The flatwoods give way to the harbor overlook, where you will see species like American oystercatcher and white ibis. Plovers, including Wilson's, black-bellied and semipalmated, roam the flats. Marbled godwits are a possibility, and winter is a good time to see white pelicans here.

Directions: From intersection of US 41, SR 768 (Jones Loop Rd.), and CR 765 (Burnt Store Rd.) south of Punta Gorda, drive appx. 11 mi. south on CR 765, turn right (W) on Durden Pkwy., and drive 1.0 mi. to the end of the road at Old Burnt Store Rd. Turn left (S) on Old Burnt Store, drive 0.5 mi. to NW 40th Ln. and turn right (W), then drive 0.5 mi. and turn left (S) on NW 44th Pl. Trailhead parking is 15 yds. on the right (yellow gate #4).

Open all year. (941) 575-5861
www.floridastateparks.org/charlotteharbor

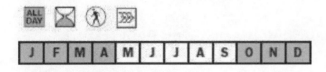

Map D
Piping Plover
Cluster

2 6 Charlotte Harbor Preserve State Park: Little Pine Island Trail

Two miles of hiking trails will lead you through this high marsh site, past interior coastal hammock and over salt flats to some isolated wetland areas. A great site for a winter visit, keep an eye out for northern harriers and palm warblers, as well as species such as blue-winged teal on the remote pond at the rear of the property. Breeding season brings common nighthawks as well as bald eagles, and the wet season (summer) provides foraging habitat for many wading species such as white ibises and roseate spoonbills. This site is within an active mitigation area, and the trails may change location from time to time due to this (as well as from seasonal flooding). Call for trail conditions and any closures, bring lots of water and insect repellent, and enjoy exploring this rare interior island site.

Directions: From intersection of SR 78 (Pine Island Rd.) and CR 765 (Burnt Store Rd.) in Cape Coral, drive 3.7 mi. west on SR 78 to parking area on right (N). From the drawbridge in the small island town of Matlacha, west of North Fort Myers, the parking area is 1.8 mi. west on the right (N).

Open all year. (941) 575-5861
www.floridastateparks.org/charlotteharbor

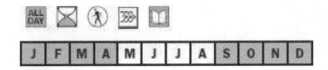

27 Cayo Costa State Park

This barrier island park is a unique experience. Board one of the commercial ferries that service the park and expect a day of birding in relatively undisturbed tranquility. As an island, this park is predominately coastal with species like American oystercatchers, black skimmers, snowy plovers and least terns to occupy your day. Magnificent frigatebirds, ospreys and bald eagles ply the open air above. Mangrove swamps and interior scrub and hammock are also on the island, so look for hawks and owls, as well as smaller birds such as buntings (indigo and painted) and warblers during spring migration. Take everything that you need for the whole day trip (there are no stores on the island) or make arrangements to spend the night in the campground if you are keen to see what is moving at first light.

Directions: The park is accessible by commercial ferry or private boat only. Commercial ferries leave from Pine Island; call park headquarters for contact information.

Open all year. (941) 964-0375
www.floridastateparks.org/cayocosta

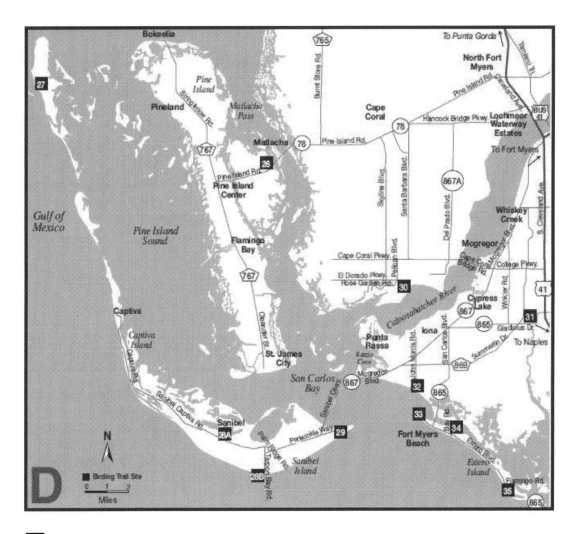

28 J. N. "Ding" Darling National Wildlife Refuge

This refuge on Sanibel Island is an internationally renowned birding destination, and for good reason – it is one of the finest wildlife refuges in the country. The Wildlife Drive will take visitors on an introductory tour of the impoundment system that makes the refuge famous, with incredible views of herons, egrets, ibises, storks and spoonbills, and shorebirds during drawdowns in spring and fall. Drive the 4-mile road slowly, or bike this same road along with several spur trails for a slower, more intimate view of the mangrove estuaries. Listen for mangrove cuckoos as you go! Put in your own canoe or kayak at one of the two unimproved ramps off Wildlife Drive for a tour of the mangrove wilderness area (no motors), or ask at the visitor center about the possibility of renting a boat or joining a boat tour. The Bailey Tract is a separate site that offers different habitat but still excellent birding. This dry barrier island interior property has a trail system that will take you through upland habitat and past freshwater inholdings that are frequented by ducks, shorebirds, sparrows, blackbirds and warblers! This is an excellent place to start or end the day, watching the flyover of larger birds between the ocean and the sound.

Directions: (A): Visitor center: cross the causeway (SR 867, $6 toll) onto Sanibel Island and turn right at the 4-way stop at Periwinkle Way. Drive 2.4 mi. and bear right onto Palm Ridge Rd. The refuge entrance is 2.3 mi. on the right (N). (B): Bailey Tract: at intersection with Palm Ridge Rd., stay straight on Periwinkle Rd., drive 0.2 mi. and turn left (S) on Tarpon Bay Rd. The entrance is 0.3 mi. on the right.

Open all year. Visitor Center: 9 a.m. to 4 p.m., May to Dec. and 9 a.m. to 5 p.m., Jan. to Mar.; Wildlife Drive: 7:30 a.m. to sunset, CLOSED FRIDAYS; Bailey Tract: dawn to dusk. (239) 472-1100
www.fws.gov/dingdarling

| J | F | M | A | M | J | J | A | S | O | N | D |

2
9 Lighthouse Park
Beach

This small site at the eastern tip of Sanibel Island is a known hotspot during migration. Be here at sunrise after weather patterns produce a large migration event and you could witness one of the most phenomenal fallouts anywhere on Florida's coastline. Late afternoons are not a bad time to visit either, as birds are moving about in anticipation of the coming flyout at sundown. Species documented at this site include 5 different vireos (including black-whiskered), more than 30 species of warblers (Cape May, Blackburnian, Wilson's and magnolia just to name a few), 7 species of flycatchers including western kingbird, several thrushes including gray-cheeked, painted and indigo buntings, blue and evening grosbeaks......the list goes on.

Directions: Cross the causeway (SR 867, $6 toll) onto Sanibel Island and turn left at the 4-way stop at Periwinkle Way. Drive 1.3 mi. to the beach access parking lot, or turn left at this lot to get to the pier/lighthouse parking.

Open all year, dawn to dusk. (239) 472-3700, (239) 472-6397
www.fortmyers-sanibel.com/listings/8530

30 Rotary Park Environmental Center

This site is predominantly mangrove estuary with a series of manmade wetlands, and is one of the only preserved green spaces in heavily-developed Cape Coral. As such, it is a magnet for species seeking out foraging areas during migration and even areas to nest during summer. The main park area offers about a mile of walking trails that loop through the mangroves around the wetlands, and pass by an observation tower that provides a commanding view of the surrounding estuary. These wetland ponds dry down at different rates, giving bird species a selection of habitat ranging from open water to mudflats. A disjunct parking area provides access to a beautiful boardwalk that takes you through mangroves and down to the mouth of the

Caloosahatchee River. Be sure to call and ask about the annual burrowing owl festival!

Directions: From intersection of Del Prado Blvd. (SR 867 A) and Cape Coral Pkwy. in Cape Coral, drive 2.4 mi. west on Cape Coral Pkwy., turn left (S) on Pelican Blvd., continue 0.9 mi. to stop sign. Turn left (E) onto El Dorado Pkwy.; make an immediate right into main park. The disjunct boardwalk parking area is straight through the stop sign, 0.8 mi. down Rose Garden Rd. on the left.

Open all year, dawn to dusk. (239) 549-4606
www.capecoral.net

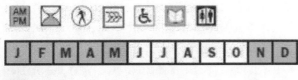

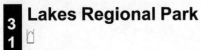

3 1 Lakes Regional Park

Although mainly recreation-oriented, this park offers boardwalks and trails around the lake that provide great views of herons and egrets, anhingas and ibises (white, glossy and scarlet). A short nature trail is worth the trip to check the quieter hammock area for skulkers such as vireos and warblers, particularly during spring and fall migrations. Also check the fragrance garden in spring for Neotropical migrants. A spring/early summer visit will reveal a very active rookery on the islands within the lake. An excellent venue for digiscoping photography – herons, egrets, ibises and anhingas raise their young here, unconcerned with the hubbub of the park.

Directions: From intersection of US 41 and SR 865 (Gladiolus Dr.) in Fort Myers, drive appx. 0.6 mi. south on SR 865 to the entrance on the right.

Open 7 a.m. to dusk, summer; 8 a.m. to 6 p.m., winter.

(239) 432-2000 www.leeparks.org

32 San Carlos Bay: Bunche Beach Preserve

This protected mangrove/beach system offers some of the best shorebirding in Lee County. Walk the beach for a mile either direction from the parking area, scanning the mangroves as well as the sand. Plovers abound – Wilson's, piping, black-bellied and semipalmated – and waders at low tide include roseate spoonbills, reddish egrets and white ibises. Watch the birds cruising above and spot least terns, as well as possible bald eagles. Low tide is the best all-around time to be here, but early morning and late evening offer a special treat as the birds come or go from their roosts in the salt flats farther inland.

Directions: From intersection of US 41 and SR 865 (Gladiolus Dr.) in Fort Myers, drive appx. 1.8 mi. south on SR 865 to Summerlin Dr. and turn left, continue appx. 5.3 mi. to John Morris Rd. and turn left again. Go 1.5 mi. to the end of the road.

Open all year, dawn to dusk. (239) 432-2158 www.leeparks.org

33 Bowditch Point Regional Park

This preserve at the northwest tip of Estero Island may be small (only 18 acres), but its location and habitat diversity make it a must-see on any birding loop that includes the island. Trails along the Gulf beach yield views of snowy, piping and Wilson's plovers, in addition to the myriad terns and gulls that cruise the beach. The bay shoreline is best for waders such as reddish egrets that poke the mudflats at low tide. Black skimmers and brown pelicans ply the surf, and occasionally a bald eagle can be seen among the ospreys overhead. Take care not to disturb loafing plovers in the dunes. Interior trails lead to a tidal creek, which is a magnet for migrating passerines – look in the sea grapes first thing in the morning for best results.

Directions: From intersection of SR 865/Estero Blvd. and San Carlos Blvd. in Fort Myers Beach, drive 0.9 mi. north on Estero Blvd. to the parking area at the end of the road.

Open all year, 7 a.m. to dusk. (239) 432-2158 www.leeparks.org

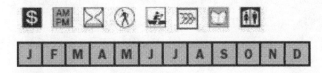

3 4 Matanzas Pass Preserve

This site encompasses not only the last remaining stand of maritime tropical hammock on Estero Island, but also supports all 3 species of mangrove (black, white and red) in close proximity, which is highly unusual. Boardwalk trails through this preserve lead through the mangroves (watch for palm warblers and blue-gray gnatcatchers) to an overlook at Estero Bay. Low tide here brings great views of wading birds including reddish egrets and white ibises, as well as shorebirds (spotted sandpiper!) on the mudflats. Continue on the trails and pass through uplands and a small, restored palm savannah where sparrows and kestrels congregate. This site is an often-overlooked jewel.

Directions: From intersection of SR 865/Estero Blvd. and San Carlos Blvd. in Fort Myers Beach, drive 1.1 mi. south on SR 865/Estero Blvd. and turn left (E) on Bay Rd. The parking area is 100 yds. ahead at the end of the road.

Open all year, sunrise to sunset. (239) 432-2158 www.leeparks.org

35 Little Estero Island Critical Wildlife Area

Walk south on the beach from the parking area and you will find a mangrove- and sea grape-lined lagoon, which hosts waders such as reddish egrets, roseate spoonbills and clapper rails. Palm warblers forage in the sand near the vegetation (an unusual sight) and merlins and peregrine falcons utilize the cover to stage hunting forays. The beach is a resting area for many species of terns, gulls, sandpipers and more. Wilson's, snowy and piping plovers, least terns, and occasionally roseate terns, among others, can be found here. The designation of this site as a state critical wildlife area requires special attention from visitors. Species of special concern, some federally threatened and endangered, nest here and others use the area as a migratory stopover or loafing area. Please do not approach shorebirds too closely, and please heed beach closures around nesting colonies.

Directions: From intersection of SR 865/Estero Blvd. and San Carlos Blvd. in Fort Myers Beach (immediately after crossing the "sky bridge"), drive 3.7 mi. south on SR 865/Estero Blvd. to the beach access parking area on the right at Flamingo Rd. The preserve begins about 0.5 mi. south down the beach.

Open all year, 24 hours/day. (239) 765-0202 ext. 136

Map E
Wood Stork Cluster

3 6 Lovers Key State Park

This park encompasses habitats ranging from Estero Bay mudflats to the Gulf of Mexico beach, with the area in between including tidal creeks and lagoons, mangrove swamps and tropical hammock. Walk the trail loops on Black Island through the hammock for red-shouldered hawks, bald eagles and osprey overhead. Low tide is best at the bay, where wading birds such as roseate spoonbills and reddish egrets will be seen. The Gulf beach is an active nesting area for snowy plovers and least terns; piping plovers winter here. Please respect beach closures! Bring your own kayak or rent one here and put in on the Great Calusa Blueway (no overnight camping here).

Directions: From the north: from intersection of SR 865/Estero Blvd. and San Carlos Blvd. in Fort Myers Beach, drive 7.3 mi. south on SR 865/Estero Blvd. to the entrance on the right (W). From the south: from intersection of US 41 and SR 865 (Bonita Beach Rd.) in Bonita Springs, drive 2.3 mi. west on SR 865 and bear right (N) onto Estero Blvd. (still SR 865). The entrance is 4.6 mi. on the left (W).

Open all year, 8 a.m. to sunset. (239) 463-4588
www.floridastateparks.org/loverskey

37 Estero Bay Preserve State Park

Bring lots of water and let the 9.5 miles of trails at this site take you through many habitats, including pine flatwoods, oak scrub, mangrove swamp, coastal dunes and isolated cypress domes. The Estero River borders this property on its south end (bring your canoe!) and the trails wind through protected land leading out to Estero Bay. Just about any group of birds you could imagine has habitat here: waders and terns at the bay; kingfishers, swallows and flycatchers at the river; woodpeckers, hawks and sparrows in the flatwoods; warblers in the cypress domes. Swallow-tailed kites cruise over during spring, and bald eagles are a known breeding species. Call ahead for ADA trail access.

Directions: From intersection of US 41 and Broadway Rd. in Estero, drive 1.4 mi. west on Broadway to trailhead parking on right.

Open all year, 8 a.m. to sunset. (239) 992-0311
www.floridastateparks.org/esterobay

38 Six Mile Cypress Slough Preserve

If you have been looking for an astounding birding experience within a major metropolitan area in South Florida, this is it. With characteristics of much larger and more well-known sites nearby, this site offers some of the best birding around. The 1.2-mile boardwalk invites you to walk slowly and silently through the freshwater swamp and hardwood hammocks, watching at close range as everything from wading birds to warblers forage in the water and woodlands around you. Blinds and viewing platforms offer places to sit for long periods and observe. Roving volunteers provide education and optics. Take your time here and enjoy the small-scale majesty of a site that rivals the more famous boardwalks in Florida.

Directions: From I-75 exit 131 (CR 876/Daniels Pkwy.) south of Fort Myers, drive 2.7 mi. west on CR 876 and turn right (N) on SR 865 (Ben C. Pratt/Six Mile Cypress Pkwy.). The entrance is 1.8 mi. on the right (E) at Penzance Blvd.

Open all year, dawn to dusk.
(239) 533-7550 www.leeparks.org

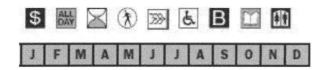

39 Hickey's Creek Mitigation Park

This site offers everything from open, scrubby flatwoods to lush hardwoods along Hickey's Creek itself. Follow the Palmetto Pines Trail for your best chance to see the small population of Florida scrub-jays that calls this park home. The North Marsh Trail leads to overlooks on a wetland, good for a variety of waders and swallows. Hickey's Creek Trail is phenomenal for warblers during migration, as it winds its way alongside this tributary of the Caloosahatchee River. Speaking of which, bring your canoe or kayak and put in (be prepared to carry it 0.5 miles) on this small tributary, follow it to the river itself, and cross over (carefully!) to Caloosahatchee Regional Park (site #40) for a full day of birding and boating!

Directions: From I-75 exit 141 (SR 80, Palm Beach Rd.) in Fort Myers, drive 8.6 mi. east on SR 80 to the entrance on the right (S).

Open all year, 7 a.m. to 6 p.m. (239) 694-0398
www.leeparks.org

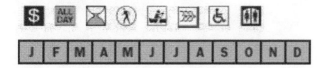

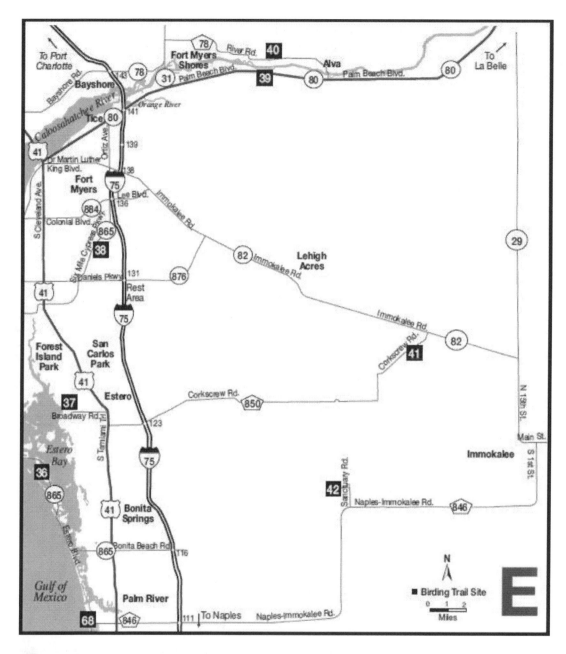

4 0 Caloosahatchee Regional Park

Offering pine flatwoods, scrub and bottomland hardwood forest along 1.3 miles of the Caloosahatchee River, the diversity of habitats in this park guarantees an impressive species list. Walk the trails on the south side of CR 78 (River Rd.), passing through dense hardwoods to the river overlooks and canoe launch (look for swallows). Put in a canoe or kayak here and tool along the shore or cross the river (carefully!) and visit Hickey's Creek Mitigation Park (site #39) on the south side of the river. Connecting trails to the west from the overlooks will bring you to an impressive stand of flatwoods, which are good for red-shouldered hawks and barred owls. Wild turkey and swallow-tailed kites can be found from the trails on the north side of the road, but watch for mountain bikes and horses in that section of the park.

Directions: From I-75 exit 143 (SR 78, Bayshore Rd.) in North Fort Myers, drive 11.8 mi. east on Bayshore/SR 78/CR 78/River Rd. to park entrance on the right (S).

Open all year, 7 a.m. to sunset. (239) 694-0398 www.leeparks.org

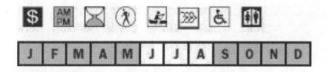

41 CREW Corkscrew Marsh Unit

Besides just being an excellent place to hike, this site offers a great introduction to the myriad habitats of the Corkscrew Regional Ecosystem Watershed (CREW). Trail loops ranging from 0.3 to 3.0 miles wind through pine flatwoods, oak hammocks, popash slough and sawgrass marsh. Observation decks offer elevated views into the marsh where the swallows and wading birds are sometimes joined by snail kites and bald eagles. Swallow-tailed kites nest here each spring, and the large trees in the hammocks give shelter to many woodpeckers and flycatchers and provide an interesting place for warbler fallout during migrations.

Directions: From intersection of SR 29 and CR 846 (Naples-Immokalee Rd.) in Immokalee, drive 5.5 mi. north on SR 29 and turn left (W) on SR 82. After 5.3 mi., turn left (SW) on CR 850 (Corkscrew Rd.); trailhead parking is 1.5 mi. on the left (S).

Open all year, sunrise to sunset. (239) 657-2253
www.crewtrust.org

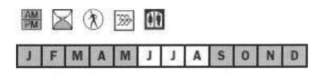

Corkscrew Swamp Sanctuary
4
2 _Gateway_*_

This Audubon Society keystone site encompasses the largest remaining stand of old-growth bald cypress on the continent, and the birds love it! Boasting a 200+ species list, the 2.25-mile boardwalk through this rare habitat is an easy walk where wildlife viewing and the appreciation of nature is paramount. Barred owls and red-shouldered hawks will watch you from low perches as you walk, while limpkins, white ibises, and the whole menagerie of egrets and herons (including night-herons!) pick their way through the shallow swamp waters. For those who want to chase the smaller birds, warblers and vireos are abundant and painted buntings are regulars during the winter. A section of the boardwalk is re-routed around a wood stork rookery during breeding season. Stop inside the Blair Audubon Center, where you can pick the brains of volunteer naturalists, browse the recent sightings, check out a pair of binoculars or simply wait out a passing rainstorm. This site is a true gem.

Directions: From Immokalee: from intersection of SR 29 and CR 846 (Naples-Immokalee Rd.), drive 13.9 mi. west on CR 846 and turn right on Sanctuary Rd.; entrance is 1.5 miles on the right. From Naples: from I-75 exit 111 (CR 846, Naples-Immokalee Rd.), drive 15.3 mi. east on CR 846 and turn left on Sanctuary Rd; entrance is 1.5 mi. on the right.

Open 7 a.m. to 7:30 p.m., Apr. 11 to Sep. 30; 7 a.m. to 5:30 p.m., Oct. 1 to Apr. 10. (239) 348-9151 www.corkscrew.audubon.org
* see "Gateways" on page 2 for more information.

Map F
Short-tailed Hawk
Cluster

4 3 Fisheating Creek Wildlife Management Area – East

An outstanding experience awaits you at this WMA. Parking, restrooms and a viewing platform along Fisheating Creek are available. As you walk along the 1.5-mile trail to Fort Center, scan the pastures on both sides for crested caracara. Also keep watch for meadowlarks, sparrows and wild turkey, plus red-shouldered and short-tailed hawks above. The vast floodplain marsh can be good for a variety of wading birds. Stately sandhill cranes are frequently spotted. Numerous duck species such as wigeon, mottled ducks and ring-necked ducks visit in winter months. In the summer, look aloft for graceful swallow-tailed kites. This is one of the largest pre-migration staging grounds in the country for this species.

Directions: From intersection of US 27 and SR 78 in Moore Haven, drive 8.5 mi. north on SR 78 and turn left (W) on Banana Grove Rd. The parking area is 1.0 mi. ahead.

Open all year. (863) 946-1194
MyFWC.com/viewing/recreation/wmas/lead/fisheating-creek/

| J | F | M | A | M | J | J | A | S | O | N | D |

4 Fisheating Creek Wildlife Management Area – West

4

This site offers a one-of-a-kind opportunity to bird in some of the most beautiful parts of rural Glades County. Rent a canoe or bring your own, secure a shuttle from the Palmdale Campground and paddle slowly down Fisheating Creek through pristine cypress swamp. Enjoy views of herons and egrets so close you won't need binoculars, palm and yellow-rumped warblers that land on the gunwale of your boat, and dozens and dozens of swallow-tailed kites wheeling overhead. Red-shouldered hawks and belted kingfishers announce your presence loudly as wood storks and common moorhens watch silently as you drift by. Water levels vary widely with rainfall, so be sure to call ahead. Opportunities range from a half-day float to a multi-day trip; call the campground [(863) 675-5999] to make arrangements.

Directions: From Moore Haven, drive 17 mi. north on US 27 to the campground on the left (W) at Palmdale, 1.0 mi. past the intersection of US 27 and SR 29.

Open all year. (863) 946-1194
MyFWC.com/viewing/recreation/wmas

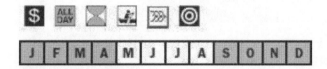

Okaloacoochee Slough State Forest and Wildlife Management Area

The 35,000 acres of this jointly-managed property encompass many different habitat types: freshwater swamp offers wading birds such as glossy ibis, wood stork, and many herons and egrets; pine flatwoods hold warblers and woodpeckers and Bachman's sparrows; and wet prairies provide views of wild turkey, sandhill cranes and hunting northern harriers. Stop at the kiosks for a map showing more than 40 miles of driving and hiking trails, and drive or bike the road system keeping an eye out for crested caracara and the occasional limpkin or bittern.

Directions: From intersection of SR 29 and CR 846 in Immokalee, drive 13.1 mi. north on SR 29 and turn right (E) on CR 832 (Keri Rd.); state forest headquarters office is 6.4 mi. on right (S). All major access roads into the forest and WMA are appx. 1.0 mi. apart along CR 832 in both directions from the office.

Open all year, sunrise to sunset. (863) 612-0776
www.fl-dof.com and
MyFWC.com/viewing/recreation/wmas

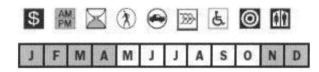

Dinner Island Ranch Wildlife Management Area

This 21,714-acre WMA and ranch has a little bit of everything: hardwood hammock, freshwater swamp, prairie and pine flatwoods. Drive or bike Hilliard Grade and walk the reclaimed cattle penning lanes watching for burrowing owls, sandhill cranes (both resident and migrant), wild turkey, crested caracara and the occasional snail kite. Oak hammocks at the ends of some trails offer warblers and vireos, and sparrows and shrikes perch in the roadside brush. The area is popular during hunting seasons. Check the website for hunt dates.

Directions: From Lake Okeechobee: from intersection of SR 80 and CR 833 south of Moore Haven, drive 17.5 mi. south on CR 833 to entrance on right (W). From Immokalee: from intersection of SR 29 and CR 846 in Immokalee, drive 19.6 mi. east on CR 846 and turn left (N) on CR 833. The entrance is 2.6 mi. on the left (W).

Open all year, dawn to dusk. (863) 902-3349
MyFWC.com/viewing/recreation/wmas/lead/dinner-island/

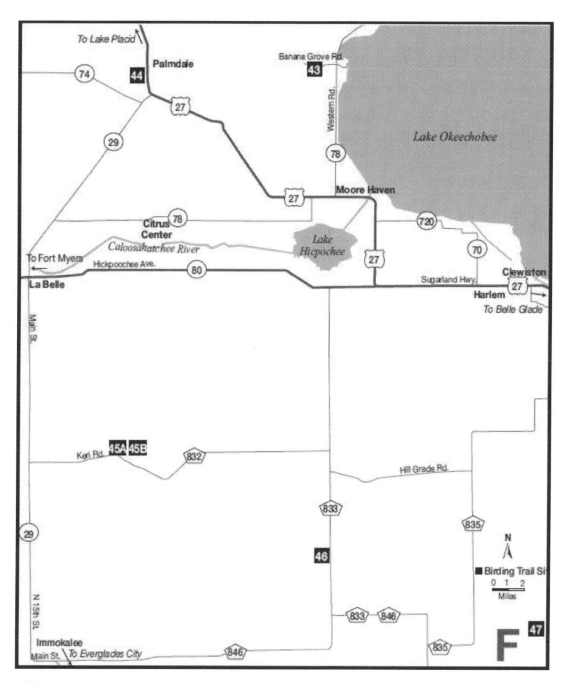

Stormwater Treatment Area 5

7

Constructed to filter agricultural runoff from water destined for the Everglades, this complex of water impoundment cells is an impressive refuge for birds and a mecca for birders all year long. Expect to see ducks such as American wigeon, lesser scaup and fulvous whistling-ducks, shorebirds like long-billed dowitcher and both yellowlegs, waders such as roseate spoonbill and glossy ibis, and occasionally other specialties like snail kite and crested caracara. Access is currently restricted to guided tours through Hendry-Glades Audubon. Public access facilities are planned.

Directions: Provided upon making a reservation for a scheduled tour. Call (863) 674-0695 for reservations.

Open on guided tours only. 1-866-433-6312
www.sfwmd.gov, www.hendrygladesaudubon.org

Map G
Okeechobee
Cluster

4
8 **Stormwater Treatment Area 1 West**

STA 1W is an integral part of the water-moving network from Lake Okeechobee to the Everglades, located at the northern tip of Loxahatchee National Wildlife Refuge (site #81). Despite the very precise technical purpose of these man-made filter marshes, this area has become an important refuge for clouds of waterbirds including American coots, roseate spoonbills, fulvous whistling-ducks, wintering shorebirds and white pelicans. A 200-foot viewing platform (with gazebos) makes observation easy (a scope is helpful). You may also hike or bike the 3-mile levee trail to see more wildlife. Area is closed during hunting season; check websites for schedules.

Directions: From I-95 in West Palm Beach, take exit 68 and drive 19.6 mi. west on SR 80 to the intersection with CR 880/Canal St. Turn left (SE) on CR 880, cross a green metal bridge and continue west for 2.7 mi. to the entrance.

Open Fri.-Mon, 6 a.m. to 8:30 p.m. except during hunts.
1-866-433-6312 www.sfwmd.gov, MyFWC.com/hunting

Royal Palm Beach Pines Natural

4 9 Area

This 773-acre flatwoods site includes an extensive trail system that winds through flatwoods maintained with regular prescribed fire, punctuated by small ephemeral marshes. Cooler months are the best for exploring this tract, watching for bald eagle, osprey and great horned owls, as well as roving flocks of wintering songbirds such as palm and prairie warblers, in the pines overhead. Tree swallows feed over the wetlands and eastern phoebes perch at the edges, strike out after flying insects, and return to their spots. Watch the pine snags for American kestrel and woodpeckers including pileated, downy and red-bellied.

Directions: From intersection of SR 704 (Okeechobee Blvd.) and SR 7 west of West Palm Beach, drive appx. 2.4 mi. west and turn right (N) on Crestwood Blvd., then drive 1.5 mi. and turn left (W) onto Saratoga Blvd. After 0.6 miles, turn left again on Natures Way; site entrance is 0.2 mi. at end of road.

Open year-round, dawn to dusk. (561) 233-2400
www.pbcgov.com/erm/natural

5 0 City of West Palm Beach Grassy Waters Preserve

This water catchment area for West Palm Beach covers 20 square miles of glades-like wetlands. Snail kites are common here, as are glossy and white ibises, limpkins and more. Bald eagles nest here as well. Several options for exploring the area include: (1) From the parking area, walk the 0.65-mile ADA boardwalk through a cypress swamp to the water, watching for songbirds like Blackburnian and yellow-rumped warblers on migration; (2) Call ahead to join a scheduled, guided "swamp tromp" or canoe/kayak trip of the area; (3) Hike or bike the 16.6-mile Owahee Trail, and hike the Apoxee (2.5 mi.) and Eagle (0.5 mi.) Trails.

Directions: From intersection of SR 710 (Beeline Hwy.) and CR 809-A (Northlake Blvd.) west of North Palm Beach, drive 1.2 mi. west on CR 809-A to the site entrance on the left (S).

Open Mon.-Sat. 8 a.m. to 4:30 p.m.; Sun. 8:30 a.m. to 5 p.m. (561) 804-4985 www.wpb.org, www.grassywaterspreserve.com

 51 Sweetbay Natural Area

Access to this large property is limited to only a small segment, including a paved trail through thick pine flatwoods to a wetland overlook. Check the wetland for waders like little blue herons, and be on the lookout for pine warblers and other flatwoods denizens. However, this site's main strength is its reliable Bachman's sparrows. They are present year-round, but most easily found in spring, when males sing in the morning, defending their territories. Listen for their "here-kitty-kitty-kitty-kitty" call February-April in particular.

Directions From intersection of SR 710 (Beeline Hwy.) and CR 809-A (Northlake Blvd.) west of North Palm Beach, drive appx. 6 mi. northwest on SR 710 and turn left (S) on Aviation Blvd.; site is on right side of road.

Open year-round, dawn to dusk. (561) 233-2400 www.pbcgov.com/erm

52 J. W. Corbett Wildlife Management Area

Portions of this 60,000-plus-acre conservation area are quite rugged. The main route described below is generally passable in 2WD vehicles though 4WD is necessary if venturing off onto other numbered trails and roads. From the south entrance, follow the signs to the Hungryland Boardwalk. This 1.3-mile walk through cypress domes and pine flatwoods is good for wood storks as well as upland species like turkeys, common yellowthroats, barred owls and more. From this point, you can hike a portion of the Florida Trail, or else drive the 25-mile circuit along Stumpers Grade south to the M-O Canal, west along the canal to South Grade, NW to North Grade, and exit onto Beeline Hwy. This route will take you through a mosaic of very wild flatwoods and wetlands good for sandhill cranes, roving flocks of wintering songbirds and woodpeckers, and raptors like red-shouldered hawks hunting from the tree line. This WMA is home to the most southeastern population of red-cockaded woodpeckers (check trails #14, 15, and N section of #8). This area is busy with hunting seasons in the fall, so spring is a better choice for birding. Check website for hunt dates.

Directions: South entrance: from intersection of SR 710 (Beeline Hwy.) and CR 809-A (Northlake Blvd.), go appx. 8.5 mi. west on CR 809-A. Turn right (N) on Pratt-Whitney Rd.; entrance is 3 mi. down this dirt road. North entrance: from intersection of SR 706 (Indiantown Rd.) and SR 710 (Beeline Hwy.) west of Jupiter, go north on SR 710 for 500 yds. to entrance on left (W).

Open all year, 24 hrs/day; closed two weeks prior to archery season. (561) 624-6989

MyFWC.com/viewing/recreation/wmas/lead/jw-corbett/

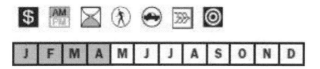

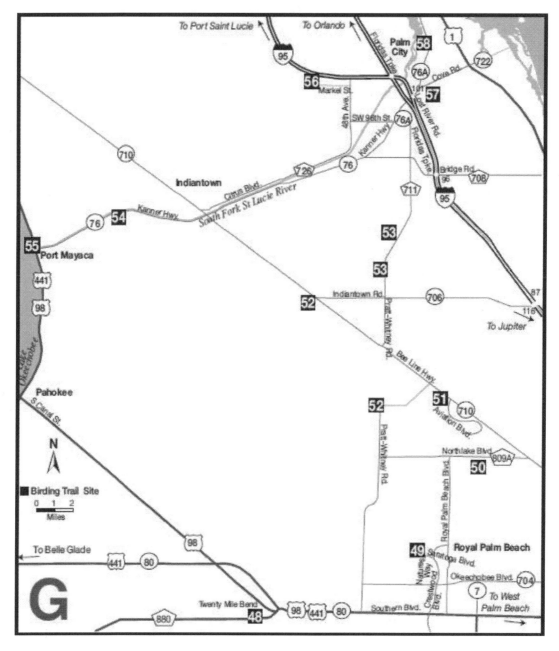

5 3 John C. and Mariana Jones/Hungryland Wildlife and Environmental Area

Off the south side of Canal 6, appx. 1.3 miles inside the main entrance, bird the West Jupiter Wetlands Trail through wetlands and flatwoods where Bachman's sparrows, snail kites and sandhill cranes are possible (expect wet feet 1 mile in). Along Canal 6, kingfishers and red-shouldered hawks are common. At the pond inside Gate 2, limpkins are likely. The Old Jupiter-Indiantown Grade trail offers various wading birds. Birding is best in cooler months as wetlands begin to dry up. Check website for hunt dates.

Directions: From intersection of SR 706 (Indiantown Rd.) and CR 711 (Pratt-Whitney Rd.) west of Jupiter, drive north on CR 711 1.5 mi. to main entrance on left (W). Old Jupiter-Indiantown Grade trail and Gate 2 are 2.5 mi. farther north.

Open all year, 24 hours/day. (561) 625-5122
MyFWC.com/viewing/recreation/wmas/lead/jones-hungryland/

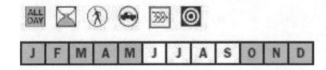

5 4 John G. and Susan H. DuPuis, Jr. Wildlife and Environmental Area

This vast property has mesic oak hammock, pine flatwoods and wetland habitats. Stop at the visitor center (look for spring/fall migrants plus buntings in winter) for a map and then drive the auto tour route (15 miles roundtrip) south along Jim Lake Grade, checking wetlands for eastern phoebes and pines for wild turkeys. At DuPuis Grade, turn left (S) and go several miles to the fishing pier area. Along the way, bird the roadside; red-cockaded woodpeckers are here. The Group Campground area has large oaks attractive to songbirds. Bald eagles are seen during the nesting season. Trails are extensive; bring water, insect repellent and a map. Check the websites for hunt dates.

Directions From the intersection of CR 710 and SR 76 (Kanner Hwy.) in Indiantown, drive west 5.4 mi. on Kanner Hwy. to the driving access entrance to DuPuis WEA on the left (S) side of the road. Hiking trailhead is 0.9 mi. farther west on the left (S). Visitor center is 1.6 mi. west of hiking trailhead, also on the left (S) side.

Open 24 hours, all year, except during deer, hog and turkey hunts.

(561) 924-5310 www.sfwmd.gov and
MyFWC.com/viewing/recreation/wmas/cooperative/dupuis

Lake Okeechobee Ridge Park: Rafael Sanchez Trail

5
5

This unconventional conservation site is a narrow strip of tropical hardwood hammock with a 6-mile trail sandwiched between expansive sugar cane fields to the east and the cleared area of the Herbert Hoover Dike to the west. This small forested ridge is thought to be the historic shoreline of Lake Okeechobee before the dike's construction, and contains large, old trees that offer a glimpse of what this area might have looked like 100 years ago. Migrating songbirds find welcome respite from sugar cane and the open water of the "Big Lake" in this long, narrow strip of hammock, and can be concentrated in significant numbers in migratory months. While in the area, keep your eyes peeled in the evenings for barn owls common in this region; the port is also worth checking for wintering white pelicans and other waterbirds.

Directions: From intersection of US 98/441 and SR 76 (Kanner Hwy.) in Port Mayaca, drive 100 yds. north on US 98/441 (across the bridge) and turn left at your first opportunity. The access road will run back toward the river, where you can turn left and park under the bridge. Enter trail at the hammock to the east of the bridge.

Open all year, dawn to dusk. (772) 220-7114 www.floridatrail.org

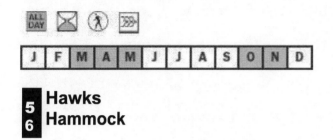

56 Hawks Hammock

This rustic site offers miles of trails through pine flatwoods frequented by hairy and downy woodpeckers, and along an extensive marsh used by sandhill cranes and endangered wood storks. At the parking area, check the canal for waterbirds and then explore the trail system, keeping an eye peeled for roaming flocks of songbirds like pine warblers. Eastern phoebes and great crested flycatchers ply their trade from fence posts and high perches, in season. The dirt road entrance can get muddy, but normally remains passable.

Directions: From intersection of SR 76 (Kanner Hwy.) and SR 76A (SW 96th St.) southwest of Stuart, drive 2.4 mi. west on SR 76A, turn right (N) on 48th Ave. and drive 1.9 mi., then turn left (W) on Markel St. and drive 2.1 mi. Park is at the end of the road.

Open all year, dawn to dusk. (772) 220-7114 www.martin.fl.us

57 Halpatiokee Regional Park

At the back of this ballpark are nature trails winding through xeric oak hammock, down to the edge of the South Fork of the St. Lucie River. This site is worth checking in migration, as well as in winter, for roving mixed feeding flocks of songbirds like northern parulas and black-and-white warblers. The trail system is extensive, so stick to the river trails where birds are most likely to follow the ecotone between habitat types.

Directions From intersection of SR 76 (Kanner Hwy.) and SR 722 (Cove Rd.) south of Stuart, drive 0.3 mi. south on SR 76 and turn left onto Lost River Rd. (before reaching I-95); park entrance is on the left.

Open all year, dawn to dusk. (772) 220-7114 www.martin.fl.us

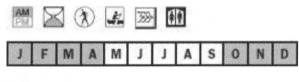

| J | F | M | A | M | J | J | A | S | O | N | D |

58 Kiplinger Nature Preserve

This Martin County Environmental Land offers a nice mosaic of habitats like scrub and wet prairie, punctuated with bayheads. These ecotones between habitat types can be particularly productive birding for wintering songbirds. Be sure to check the pine snags in the eastern scrub area for woodpeckers and hawks, and the mangrove edge along the North Trail for waders. Give the wet prairie a wide berth in late spring, so as not to disturb nesting sandhill cranes.

Directions From intersection of SR 76 (Kanner Hwy.) and SR 722 (Cove Rd.) south of Stuart, drive north on SR 76 for appx. 3.0 mi. to the entrance on the left (W).

Open all year, dawn to dusk. (772) 220-7114 www.martin.fl.us

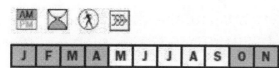

Map H
Spoonbill
Cluster

5 Rocky Point Hammock
9 Park

This site is a pocket of hammock and sand pine scrub surrounded by suburban development. Its shady live oak-hickory canopy is blanketed in resurrection fern, and one look is all you need to understand why migrants like northern parula, black-and-white and yellow-throated warblers take refuge here. The understory is healthy, native and just open enough to tempt you to look for skulking thrushes and ovenbirds. On good migration days this is a hotbed of feeding songbirds. On slower days expect a short, pleasant walk through magical old live oaks.

Directions: From intersection of US 1 and SR 722 (Cove Rd.) south of Stuart, drive 1.4 mi. east on SR 722 and turn left (N) on Manatee Cove Rd. After 0.5 mi., turn right (E) on Horseshoe Point Rd., drive 0.8 mi. and turn left (N) on Kubin Ave. The park entrance is 5 mi. on the left.

Open all year, dawn to dusk. (772) 220-7114 www.martin.fl.us

| J | F | M | A | M | J | J | A | S | O | N | D |

6 St. Lucie Inlet Preserve State
0 Park

This remote park occupies the northern end of the peninsula (Jupiter Island), which it shares with Hobe Sound National Wildlife Refuge (site #62). For all its accessibility, though, it may as well be an island, offering one of the most remote beach experiences left in this part of the state. Boardwalks through the mangroves can be good for mangrove cuckoos in summer and migrants in fall and winter. The beach is pristine and offers a stark contrast to the development of Hutchinson Island to the north across the inlet. Plovers, gulls and terns use the beach and occasionally, wintering purple sandpipers turn up on the northern jetty. The only access for this property is by boat, and there are no nearby concessionaires. Bring your canoe or kayak and launch from the park at the end of SR 722. Paddle the unmarked canoe trail through the mangroves or tie up at the park's extensive dock. A beautiful place to bird...worth the challenge of getting there.

Directions: From intersection of US 1 and SR 722 (Cove Rd.) south of Stuart, drive 2.5 mi. east on SR 722 to the end. The park is on the other side of the Intracoastal Waterway.

Open year-round, 8 a.m. to sunset. (772) 219-1880
www.floridastateparks.org/stlucieinlet

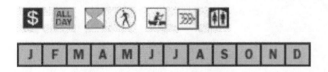

| J | F | M | A | M | J | J | A | S | O | N | D |

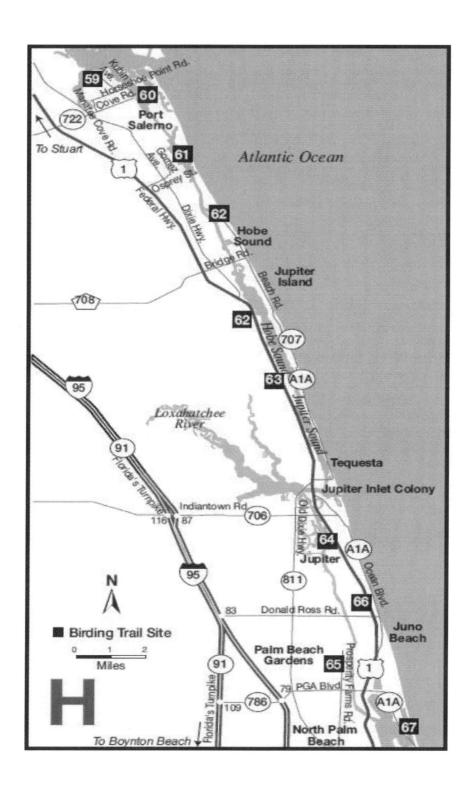

Atlantic Ocean

Port Salerno

Hobe Sound

Jupiter Island

Loxahatchee River

Tequesta

Jupiter Inlet Colony

Jupiter

Juno Beach

Palm Beach Gardens

North Palm Beach

To Stuart

To Boynton Beach

N

■ Birding Trail Site

0   1   2
Miles

H

59
60
61
62
62
63
64
65
66
67

722
1
708
95
91
706
811
786
91
95

A1A
A1A
A1A

Kubin Ave.
Horseshoe Point Rd.
Cove Rd.
Manatee Cove Rd.
Gomez Ave.
Osprey St.
Dixie Hwy.
Federal Hwy.
Bridge Rd.
Beach Rd.
Hobe Sound
Jupiter Sound
Old Dixie Hwy.
Ocean Blvd.
Indiantown Rd.
116
87
Donald Ross Rd.
83
Prosperity Farms Rd.
PGA Blvd.
79
109
Florida's Turnpike
1

61 Peck Lake Park

A linear trail departs from the NE corner of the parking lot and crosses seven habitat types from mesic flatwoods all the way down to tidal swamp at the Intracoastal Waterway. This site is worth a quick look, especially in migration, for its ease of access and diversity of habitats. Watch for migrants like skulking Swainson's warblers, just-arrived in the spring, and solitary waterbirds like spotted sandpipers in winter at the water's edge.

Directions: Fom intersection of US 1 and CR 708 (Bridge Rd.) in Hobe Sound, drive 3.4 mi. north on US 1, turn right (E) on Osprey St., drive 0.7 mi. and turn left (N) on Gomez Ave. The park entrance is on the right (E).

Open all year, dawn to dusk. (772) 220-7114 www.martin.fl.us

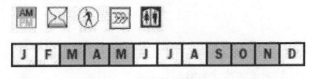

62 Hobe Sound National Wildlife Refuge

This refuge has two very different access points for exploration. At the Headquarters on US 1, trails wind through coastal scrub down to a sugar sand beach, lined with mangroves at the Intracoastal Waterway, where you can watch for waders like yellow-crowned night-herons, soaring osprey and foraging least terns overhead. In the scrub in October and April, listen for songbirds like black-throated blue warblers foraging just prior to departing on, or just after returning from their long overwater migrations. The beach access on Jupiter Island offers one of the last undeveloped stretches of Atlantic beachfront in South Florida. Watch for shorebirds like Wilson's plover, loons and gannets in winter, and frigatebirds overhead in summer. You may also see the marked nests of sea turtles as you enjoy the natural beauty of this area.

Directions: Beach: from intersection of US 1 and CR 708 (Bridge Rd.) in Hobe Sound, drive east on CR 708 appx. 1.4 mi. and turn left (N) on N. Beach Rd.; beach access is 1.5 mi. ahead. Headquarters: from intersection of US 1 and CR 708 (Bridge Rd.) in Hobe Sound, drive appx. 2 mi. south on US 1 to entrance on left.

Open all year, dawn to dusk. (772) 546-6141. Contact Nature Center at (772) 546-2067 for guided walks and educational programs. www.fws.gov/hobesound

63 Jonathan Dickinson State Park

There are birds to see year-round at this extensive property, but the experience is most comfortable in the cooler weather months. Regardless, the site offers miles of trails through flatwoods and scrub (ask at the ranger station for scrub-jay locations). It also includes a boat concession at the Loxahatchee River, where you can take a guided motorboat tour, or rent a canoe for yourself. The upper reaches of the river are intimate and secluded, offering good opportunities for good looks at little blue herons, least bitterns and wintering northern waterthrushes. Watch for bald eagles and common nighthawks in the sky and wild turkeys on the roadsides.

Directions: From intersection of US 1 and CR 708 (Bridge Rd.) in Hobe Sound, drive south on US 1, 4.6 mi. to entrance on right.

Open all year, 8 AM to sunset. (772) 546-2771
www.floridastateparks.org/jonathandickinson

6 4 Jupiter Ridge Natural Area

This scrub habitat site has some serious topography for Florida, with very hilly sections on its south loop. For birding purposes, follow the paved trail to the wetland overlook (and check for vagrants and migrants; a black-faced grassquit was present here in 2004). From the overlook, pick up the sand trail to Ski Beach. The scrub surrounding this trail and Ski Beach are the most likely locations on the property to view threatened Florida scrub-jays.

Directions: From intersection of US 1 and SR 706 (Indiantown Rd.) in Jupiter, drive 1.3 mi. south on US 1; entrance is on the right (W).

Open all year, dawn to dusk. (561) 233-2400
www.pbcgov.com/erm/natural

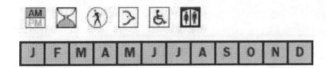

J F M A M J J A S O N D

6 5 Frenchman's Forest Natural Area

This lovely site in busy Palm Beach Gardens is filled with big old live oaks and sabal palms, traversed by an old-growth cypress strand. This mosaic of habitats is excellent not only for migratory songbirds but also for residents like great horned owls and pileated woodpeckers. A vagrant black-faced grassquit was found at this location in 2004, so who knows what a birding excursion here will turn up? The ADA trail offers good access, and the red trail also provides entrée to the hardwood swamp via boardwalk.

Directions: From intersection of US 1/SR A1A, and SR 786 (PGA Blvd.) in North Palm Beach, drive 0.9 mi. west on SR 786 and turn right (N) on Prosperity Farms Rd. The site entrance is 0.7 mi. on the left (W), just north of the canal bridge.

Open all year, dawn to dusk. (561) 233-2400
www.pbcgov.com/erm/natural

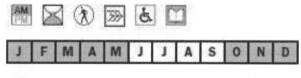

66 Juno Dunes Natural Area

This property has two portions, Oceanfront and West, the latter of which is the most rewarding to bird. While scrub may not have the highest diversity of birdlife, it is home to Florida's only endemic bird species, the Florida scrub-jay. Several families live on the portion of this property west of US 1. From the parking lot, look north and south along US 1 on power lines, posts and other lookouts for jays sitting sentinel over their territories, or walk the sandy trail that leads north through this portion of the property. The paved trail leads to an overlook of a wetland worth checking for waders or skulking migrants.

Directions: From intersection of US 1 and Donald Ross Rd. in Juno Beach, drive north on US 1 for 0.2 mi. to Loggerhead Park and turn right (E) for Oceanfront Trail access. To reach the West Trail entrance, go 0.3 mi. farther north on US 1, make a U-turn, and go south for 0.1 mi. to parking area on west side of US 1 (southbound access only).

Open all year, dawn to dusk. (561) 233-2400
www.pbcgov.com/erm/natural

6 7 John D. MacArthur Beach State Park

At the northernmost parking area, bird the Satinleaf Trail for migratory songbirds in season like Kentucky warblers and ovenbirds, then walk or ride the long boardwalk across the lagoon to the beach overlooks. From overlooks in October, watch for raptors migrating down and foraging from the dune line. At low tide, flats are exposed in the lagoon, so keep an eye peeled for waders like roseate spoonbills and shorebirds. Guided paddling trips and interpretive hikes are offered regularly, so check in advance for a schedule and reservations. This site can get very busy with beachgoers, so plan accordingly.

Directions: From intersection of US 1, SR 786 (PGA Blvd.), and SR A1A (Ocean Blvd.) in North Palm Beach, drive south on A1A appx. 2.0 mi. to the entrance on the left.

Open all year, 8 a.m. to sunset. (561) 624-6950
www.floridastateparks.org/macarthurbeach

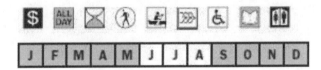

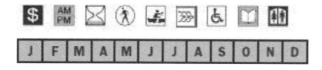

Map I
Mangrove
Cluster

6 Delnor-Wiggins Pass State Park
8

This small barrier island park offers mostly mangrove habitat with Turkey Bay on one side and a nice stretch of sea grape-lined beach on the other for variety. Low tide on the bay is great for waders and shorebirds (look for the resident yellow-crowned night-herons). Wiggins Pass is the best spot for shorebirds including loafing least terns, and bald eagles occasionally hunt there. A viewing tower at the north end of the park offers long-range views of both the pass and the beach.

Directions: From I-75 exit 111 (CR 846, Immokalee Rd.), drive 6.0 mi. west to the park entrance at the end of the road.

Open all year, 8 a.m. to sundown. (239) 597-6196
www.floridastateparks.org/delnorwiggins

J	F	M	A	M	J	J	A	S	O	N	D

6 Conservancy of Southwest Florida Nature
9 Center

This small natural oasis in downtown Naples offers habitat for a variety of species. Short nature trails through native landscaping offer sightings of woodpeckers, hawks, owls, and many warblers, thrushes and vireos during migration. Take the electric boat cruise (free with admission) through a mangrove-lined waterway to view eagles, osprey and an impressive collection of waders. An on-site rehabilitation facility with educational tours is an added bonus. This site is undergoing extensive renovations through 2012 and may be closed at times; please call ahead.

Directions: From intersection of CR 886 (Golden Gate Pkwy.) and CR 851 (Goodlette-Frank Rd.) in Naples, drive 0.5 mi. south on CR 851 and turn left (E) on 14th Ave. N.; entrance is 0.1 mi. on the left.

Call ahead for program times and hours of operation.
(239) 262-0304 www.conservancy.org

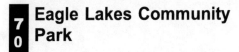

70 Eagle Lakes Community Park

This park is turning out to be a local hotspot, and is often overlooked by traveling birders. Behind the ball fields, track, and eutrophic holding pond, you will find a berm system around two very productive water reclamation ponds which host wading birds, bitterns, moorhens and gallinules, swallows, terns and gulls, and many ducks during winter. Native plantings surrounding these ponds encourage the presence of everything from blackbirds to warblers to sparrows. In the past, this site has been reliable for bronzed cowbird and Eurasian wigeon. With a checklist of 170+ extremely varied species (that grows constantly!), this site is a must-see if you're in the area.

Directions: From intersection of US 41 (Tamiami Trail) and SR 951 (Collier Blvd.) south of Naples, drive 1.2 mi. north on US 41 to the entrance on the right (E).

Open all year, 8 a.m. to dusk. (239) 252-4000 www.colliergov.net

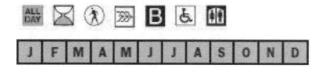

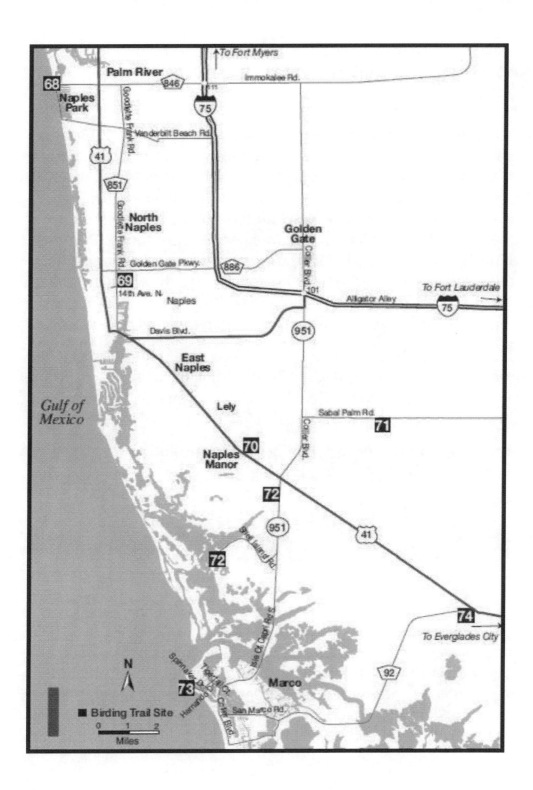

To Fort Myers

Palm River

68

846

Immokalee Rd.

Naples Park

F11

75

Goodlette Frank Rd.

Vanderbilt Beach Rd.

41

851

North Naples

Golden Gate

Golden Gate Pkwy.

886

Collier Blvd.

101

Goodlette Frank Rd.

69

14th Ave. N.

Naples

To Fort Lauderdale

Alligator Alley

75

Davis Blvd.

951

East Naples

Lely

Sabal Palm Rd.

Collier Blvd.

71

70

Naples Manor

72

951

Gulf of Mexico

41

Bird Island Rd.

72

74

To Everglades City

Isle Of Capri Rd.

92

N

Collier Blvd.

Marco

Spam ave...

Tigertail Ct.

73

Hernando Dr.

San Marco Rd.

■ Birding Trail Site

0   1   2

Miles

71 Picayune Strand State Forest: Sabal Palm Hiking Trail

This 3.2-mile trail system winds through mostly pine flatwoods and freshwater swamp, and passes some reclaimed farm fields along the way. Thanks to careful management this site not only contains all the dry upland species such as hairy woodpeckers, pine warblers and brown-headed nuthatches, it also contains one of the southernmost populations of red-cockaded woodpeckers in the country. Portions of the trail are very wet during the summer rainy season, but persistent birders who make it to the farm fields at the southern end of the trail system will be rewarded with views of white and glossy ibises, wood stork and sandhill crane. Stay on the marked trail and take lots of water at all times of day!

Directions: From I-75 exit 101 (SR 951, Collier Blvd.), drive 4.3 mi. south, turn left (E) on Sabal Palm Rd., and continue 3.2 mi. to trailhead parking on right (look for "Trailwalker" sign).

Open dawn to dark, unless camping. (239) 348-7557
www.fl-dof.com/state_forests/picayune_strand.html

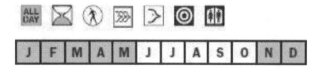

J	F	M	A	M	J	J	A	S	O	N	D

72 Rookery Bay National Estuarine Research Reserve

Start by visiting the Environmental Learning Center at the main entrance to view the interpretive exhibits. Pick up a bird list, and check the upland hammocks around the Center for warblers, woodpeckers and vireos. Shell Island Road, just a few miles from the main entrance, offers an opportunity to drive or bike through pine flatwoods and coastal scrub where you may find reintroduced Florida scrub-jays, eastern towhees and pileated woodpeckers. At the end of the road you enter a mangrove forest, where the Shell Point Canoe Trail begins (bring your own). Much of the reserve itself is accessible only by boat. The estuary offers a host of wading birds such as reddish egrets and roseate spoonbills, as well as the possibility of spotting peregrine falcons, bald eagles and mangrove cuckoos.

Directions: From intersection of US 41 (Tamiami Trail) and SR 951 (Collier Blvd.) south of Naples, drive 0.7 mi. south on SR 951 to Tower Rd. Turn right (W) and turn left (S) into parking lot. Shell Island Rd. entrance is 2.0 mi. farther south on SR 951 on the right (W).

Winter (November – May) 9 a.m. to 4 p.m., Monday – Saturday; Summer (June – October) 9 a.m. to 4 p.m., Monday – Friday
(239) 417-6310 www.rookerybay.org

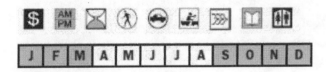

| J | F | M | A | M | J | J | A | S | O | N | D |

73 **Tigertail Beach Park**

One of the best all-around birding spots in southwest Florida. The tidal lagoon at the "beach" offers great views of shorebirds including Wilson's, piping and snowy plovers, as well as least terns, roseate spoonbills, red knots and a host of other sought-after species. Peregrine falcons ply their trade among the terns and gulls, while osprey, bald eagles and pelicans dive offshore. This corner of Marco Island is a true "hotspot" during migrations, and rarities occur here often. When visiting this site, be aware that the actual shoreline beyond the lagoon is a state-owned critical wildlife area, designed to protect the nesting colonies of some of the species of concern mentioned here. Please respect all beach closings and practice good birding etiquette.

Directions: From intersection of US 41 (Tamiami Trail) and SR 951 (Collier Blvd.) south of Naples, drive appx. 8.2 mi. south on SR 951 onto Marco Island and turn right (W) on Tigertail Ct. Continue 1.0 mi. and turn left (S) on Hernando Dr.; park entrance is 0.8 mi. ahead, where road dead-ends into Spinnaker Dr.

Open all year, 8 a.m. to sunset. (239) 252-4000
www.colliergov.net

74 Collier-Seminole State Park

The temperate zone meets the subtropics here, and this site offers many ways to explore the habitats that result. A short nature trail passes through native royal palms and offers boardwalks and a marsh overlook platform where ibises and spoonbills congregate. A 3.5-mile unpaved bike trail winds through marsh, hammock and pine flatwoods, taking you close to sparrows, warblers and summer tanagers. For the restless, 6.5 miles of backcountry hiking trails will take you through oak scrub, flatwoods and even recent burn regeneration – keep an eye out for wild turkeys. Finally, a 13.6-mile canoe trail loop winds through the mangrove estuary of the Blackwater River where osprey, kingfishers and wood storks watch you pass.

Directions: From intersection of US 41 (Tamiami Trail) and SR 951 (Collier Blvd.) south of Naples, drive 8.3 mi. east on US 41 to the main park entrance on the right (S). You will need to ask the rangers here for maps and directions to the hiking and biking trails, as well as the combinations for the gates that guard these areas.

Open all year, 8 a.m. to sundown. (239) 394-3397

www.floridastateparks.org/collierseminole

Map J
Cypress
Cluster

7 5 Fakahatchee Strand Preserve State Park

This park protects more than 85,000 acres of slowly moving fresh water that constitutes the largest strand swamp in Florida, contains the second largest tract of old-growth bald cypress, and harbors 38 species of ferns, 14 species of bromeliads and 44 species of native orchids. A) The 11-mile unpaved Janes Scenic Drive gives you access to all this habitat, and takes you through the territories of herons and egrets, swallow-tailed kites, snail kites, bald eagles and the occasional white-crowned pigeon (one of the northernmost populations of this species). B) The Big Cypress Bend Boardwalk in the southern end of the park is a half-mile trail into old-growth cypress, giving close-up looks at lots of waders, nesting bald eagles, plus warblers and vireos during migration.

Directions: A) Janes Scenic Drive: from intersection of US 41 (Tamiami Trail) and SR 29 east of Naples, drive 2.5 mi. north on SR 29 and turn left (W) on Janes Memorial Scenic Dr. Go to stop sign and turn right. Park headquarters and the start of the scenic drive are 0.9 mi. ahead. B) Big Cypress Bend Boardwalk: from intersection of US 41 (Tamiami Trail) and SR 29 east of Naples, drive 7.0 mi. west on US 41 to entrance on right (N).

Open 8 a.m. to dusk. (239) 695-4593
www.floridastateparks.org/fakahatcheestrand

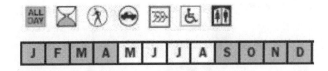

 Everglades National Park: Gulf Coast Visitor Center

Although most birders know of the many possibilities in Everglades National Park, not many are aware of this remote access that will take you into the aquatic parts of the park and the adjoining "Ten Thousand Islands" area. Narrated boat tours explore the mangrove estuary ecosystem where waders are plentiful and magnificent frigatebirds join the gulls and terns overhead. Winter brings loons and white pelicans, and the possibility of short-tailed hawks as well. Adventurous birders can either rent a kayak on-site or bring their own and explore the backwaters of Chokoloskee Bay and Turner River without a guide. With backcountry permits, you can start your odyssey down the 99-mile Wilderness Waterway that will take you all the way to Flamingo.

Directions: From intersection of US 41 (Tamiami Trail) and SR/CR 29 east of Naples, drive south on CR 29. The park entrance is 4.7 mi. on the right (W) at Oyster Bar Ln.

Open 9 a.m. to 4:30 p.m., mid April – mid November; 8 a.m. to 4:30 p.m., mid November – mid April. (239) 695-3311 www.nps.gov/ever

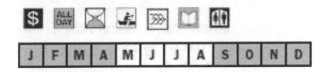

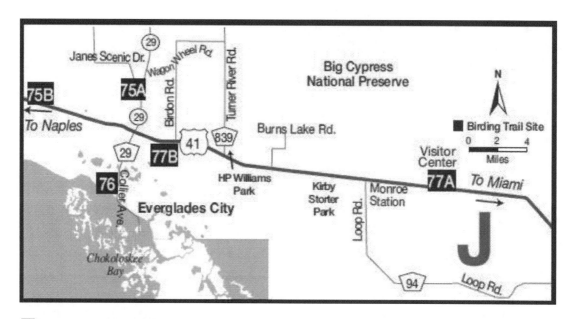

77 Big Cypress National Preserve

This expansive preserve is a good place to spend the whole day (or several days) exploring what the Everglades ecosystem and Big Cypress Swamp have to offer. Stop at either the Oasis Visitor Center or Big Cypress Swamp Welcome Center for a map and in-depth information. Loop Road (CR 94) is a 24.5-mile scenic drive with roadside, deep-swamp views of wading birds, barred owls and the occasional swallow-tailed kite flyover. The Florida National Scenic Trail starts from Loop Road and will take the restless deep into the swamp (ask ahead for trail conditions!). Short boardwalks along the water's edge at the visitor center, welcome center, Kirby Storter Roadside Park and H.P. Williams Roadside Park give close views of waders, as well as warblers, woodpeckers, flycatchers and thrushes (including bluebirds). Scenic Turner River Road (CR 839) is a 20-mile drive to Bear Island along canals and through swamp and prairie where you may see least bittern, sora, snail kite, and marsh and sedge wrens. Another great driving route is the 16-mile loop formed by CR 839, 837 (Wagon Wheel Rd.) and 841

(Birdon Rd.). As you drive from place to place, keep an eye skyward for wheeling wood storks, white ibises and roseate spoonbills. Please be advised that US 41 carries high-speed traffic, therefore inattentive driving is dangerous.

Directions: A) Oasis Visitor Center is on north side of US 41 (Tamiami Trail), appx. 21 mi. from intersection with SR 29 in the west and appx. 35 mi. from intersection with SR 997 (Krome Ave.) in the east. Other sites mentioned are within 15 mi. of the Visitor Center. B) Big Cypress Swamp Welcome Center is on south side of US 41 appx. 5 mi. east of SR 29.

Preserve open all year, 24 hours/day; Visitor and Welcome Center open all year (except Christmas) 9 a.m. to 4:30 p.m. daily.

(239) 695-1201 VC; (239) 695-4758 WC www.nps.gov/bicy

Map K
Snail Kite
Cluster

7 8 Everglades National Park: Shark Valley Visitor Center

Bike, walk or take the narrated tram tour down the 15-mile loop road that extends into this northern portion of the park's marsh ecosystem and ends at an elevated, wheelchair-accessible viewing tower. Excellent opportunities to see all the wading birds that this national park is famous for, including wood stork, roseate spoonbill, white and glossy ibis, and the uncommon great white heron. Also watch for short-tailed hawks, plus snail, white-tailed and swallow-tailed kites. Sunset is a particularly good time to be at the viewing tower, when many wading birds arrive to roost in the mangroves. Rent a bike or bring your own, or climb aboard the tram and enjoy a 2-hour tram tour narrated by a park naturalist or ranger. Bring plenty of water and insect repellent.

Directions: From intersection of US 41 (Tamiami Trail) and SR 997 (Krome Ave.) west of Miami, drive 17.3 mi. west on US 41 to entrance on left (S).

Open all year, 8:30 a.m. to 6 p.m.; Visitor Center open 9:15 a.m. to 5:15 p.m. (305) 221-8776 www.nps.gov/ever

| J | F | M | A | M | J | J | A | S | O | N | D |

■ Holey Land and Rotenberger Wildlife Management Areas

A drivable levee system is essentially the only way to access the more than 60,000 acres that make up these two Wildlife Management Areas (WMAs). Together with the 670,000 acres of adjoining Everglades and Francis S. Taylor WMA (site #80), this vast protected area constitutes one of the largest intact properties of the Everglades ecosystem. Levees along both sides of the canals that separate the properties provide opportunities to enjoy relatively uninterrupted viewing of green herons (among others), black-necked stilts, purple gallinules and common moorhens, along with occasional sightings of American bitterns and king rails. Keep an eye skyward also; it is not uncommon to see swallow-tailed and snail kites, northern harriers and bald eagles.

The L4/L5 levee system, which runs east/west approximately 21 miles, is bisected by levee roads along Miami Canal at the boundary between these two WMAs. The Miami Canal levees can also be driven, but be aware that the road on the east side has no outlet and you will have to turn around. The L4/L5 road is a long drive that ends on rural Huff Bridge Rd., far from the area where the levee road starts. It can be a long wait or a long walk in the event of car trouble. In addition, the levee roads are joined at intervals by other dirt roads, and the system can become confusing. It is advisable to obtain area maps before you go, and to fill up both your gas tank and water bottles before setting out.

Directions: From intersection of I-75 and US 27 west of Fort Lauderdale, drive 14.5 mi. north on US 27 to entrance road on left (W) at the Palm Beach/Broward County line, where the L4/L5 levee road system begins. Follow the L4/L5 road 5.75 mi. west to Holey Land WMA (A) and 14.4 mi. west to Rotenberger WMA (B).

Open all year, 24 hours/day. (954) 746-1789
MyFWC.com/viewing/recreation/wmas/lead/holey-land/
MyFWC.com/viewing/recreation/wmas/lead/rotenberger/

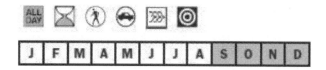

⬛ Everglades and Francis S. Taylor Wildlife Management Area ⌂
8 0

The interior of this 670,000-acre Wildlife Management Area (WMA), with its freshwater swamp and wet prairie, is inaccessible without an airboat. A drivable levee system on its northern boundary (see Holey Land and Rotenberger WMAs, site #79) and boat ramps along both US 41 in the south and I-75 across its middle offer glimpses into this huge ecosystem. True Everglades at its best, the views from the boat ramps include egrets, herons and most other wading birds, plus clouds of swallows and occasional sightings of bald eagles and swallow-tailed kites. Snail kites can be seen at the ramps along US 41.

Directions: On the north side of US 41, boat ramps are located appx. 1.3, 12, 12.5, 15 and 21 mi. west of the intersection with SR 997 (Krome Ave.) west of Miami. On I-75, interpretive kiosks and boat ramps are located appx. 8, 11, 13 and 16.5 mi. west of the intersection with US 27 west of Ft. Lauderdale, with the most developed ramp at mile marker 35. Interpretive displays of the Everglades ecosystem, picnic facilities and restrooms are located here at the Miami Canal DOT Rest Area along with an observation tower. Directions to the northern levee are described with Holey Land and Rotenberger WMAs.

Open all year, dawn to dusk. (954) 746-1789
MyFWC.com/viewing/recreation/wmas/lead/everglades/

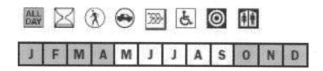

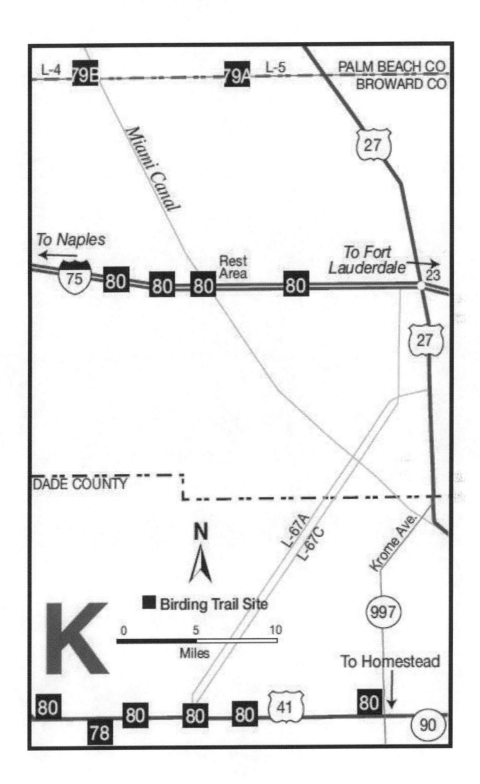

Map L
Whistling-Duck
Cluster

8 1 Arthur R. Marshall Loxahatchee National Wildlife Refuge: Headquarters Area *Gateway**

This premier birding site is a gateway with good reason: year-round, there's something to see. After passing the fee station, the Visitor Center will be on the right, with a wheelchair-accessible boardwalk through a cypress swamp. Pick up a map and bird the boardwalk and even the parking lot, for songbird migrants like wood thrush and American redstart. If instead of turning right (N) at the Visitor Center you continue west on the entrance road, you'll encounter a parking area on the left (S) at a trailhead leading to the impoundments. The eastern boundary of these impoundments can have yellow-breasted chats, painted buntings and common yellowthroats in the vegetation. Off the west side of the levees, you'll see impoundments of increasing depth as you walk south, hosting waders like limpkin, waterfowl including both blue- and green-winged teal, and secretive marsh birds like American bittern. Smooth-billed Anis are no longer found here. The Visitor Center also schedules educational programs and guided walks. Duck hunting is allowed by permit only in season (Dec. - Jan.) from the Hillsboro Area entrance.

Directions: From intersection of US 441 and SR 804 (Boynton Beach Blvd.) west of Boynton Beach, drive south on US 441 appx. 2.0 mi. Turn right (W) on Lee Rd; site entrance is at the end.

Open 6 a.m. to sunset. (561) 734-8303 www.fws.gov/loxahatchee

*see "Gateways" on page 2 for more information.

82 Green Cay Wetlands and Nature Center

This created wetland is Wakodahatchee's newer, bigger sibling. Offering more than 1.5 miles of boardwalk across open water, vegetated wetlands and mudflats, this site is just as spectacular as Wakodahatchee, only bigger! Expect both yellowlegs and peeps like least sandpiper on flats and in the shallows. Purple gallinule and least bittern will stick to the emergent vegetation. Swallows including tree, barn and northern rough-winged swirl over the water in spring, and wintering ducks love the open water in winter. An impressive, on-site nature center coordinates guided walks and classes, and interprets the surrounding wetlands for visitors. Call ahead for nature center hours of operation.

Directions: From intersection of SR 806 (Atlantic Ave.) and Hagen Ranch Rd. west of Delray Beach, drive 2.2 mi. north on Hagen Ranch Rd. to entrance on right (E).

Boardwalk open year-round, 7 a.m. to sunset.
(561) 966-7000 www.pbcparks.com/nature

83 Wakodahatchee Wetlands

These constructed wetlands were designed to recycle highly-treated wastewater from the county's Southern Region Water Reclamation Facility. In addition, they provide approximately 50 acres of freshwater marsh habitat for wetland bird species. A 0.75-mile elevated boardwalk offers unbelievable views of purple gallinule, sora, least bittern, limpkin, black-bellied whistling-ducks and more. Eye-candy birding at its best! The boardwalk is also popular with fitness walkers which can cause some vibrations for would-be photographers, but otherwise, this place is for the birds (and birders)! The site has something in all seasons and is excellent for all skill levels. A must-see in Palm Beach County.

Directions: From intersection of SR 806 (Atlantic Ave.) and Jog Rd. west of Delray Beach, drive 1.8 mi. north on Jog Rd. to entrance on right (E).

Open year-round, 7 a.m. to 7 p.m. (561) 493-6000
www.pbcgov.com/waterutilities/

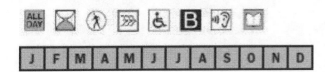

84 Seacrest Scrub Natural Area

This 54-acre remnant of sand pine scrub includes a brief ADA trail (Gopher Tortoise Nature Trail) and an additional 0.75-mile sandy trail (Sand Pine Hiking Trail). While not very big, it's a pocket of green in the middle of an otherwise urban area and gets songbirds in migration and winter. A black-throated gray warbler was seen here in February 2005, along with more common migrant species. Watch for osprey, American kestrel and pileated woodpecker. Worth checking quickly, if you're in the area.

Directions: From intersection of US 1 and SR 792 (Woolbright Rd.) in Boynton Beach, drive appx. 0.3 mi. west on SR 792 and turn left (S) on Seacrest Blvd. The site entrance is 1.4 mi. on the left (E).

Open all year, dawn to dusk. (561) 233-2400 www.pbcgov.com

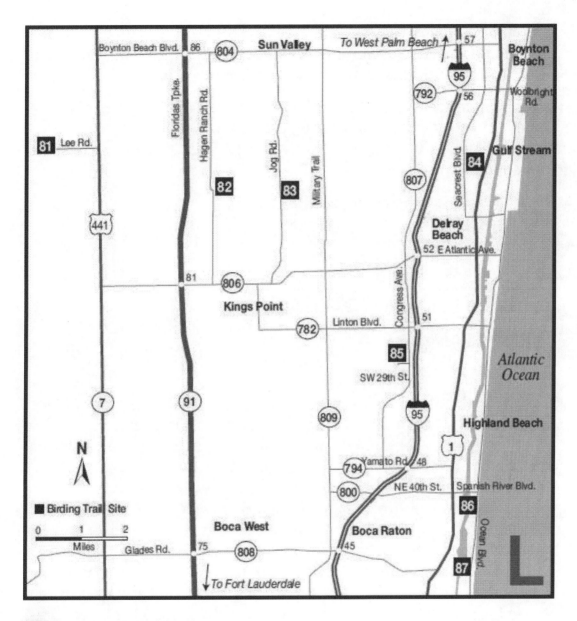

85 Delray Oaks Natural Area

Follow the paved ADA trail through the palm-oak hammock to a strand swamp and observation platform at the end, watching along the way for gray catbirds, palm warblers and other songbirds in spring/fall. The dirt path hiking trail can be worth checking for similar species. This small property is a quick visit in migration if you're in the area.

Directions: From intersection of US 1 and SR 782 (Linton Blvd.) in Delray Beach, drive 1.2 mi. west on SR 782 and turn left (S) on S. Congress Ave. Go 0.9 mi. and turn right (W) on SW 29th St.; entrance is immediately on the right.

Open all year, dawn to dusk. (561) 233-2400
www.pbcgov.com

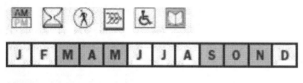

| J | F | M | A | M | J | J | A | S | O | N | D |

86 Spanish River Park

This city park has extensive parking areas and picnic pavilions under large, old ficus and gumbo limbo trees, and has a reputation as a good spot for migratory songbird fallouts as well as the occasional rarity. Best bets are birding the hiking trail that bounds the western edge of the park, checking the trees for migrants like blue-winged warblers and Swainson's thrushes (most years bring 25+ species of warbler!). The convoluted parking areas provide a lot of access to edge cover and big trees that can be worth checking for unusual flycatchers like La Sagra's and other assorted surprises. Entry fee to the park is nearly $20 per car, however, visitors are permitted to park in the metered spots on Ocean Rd., and walk into the park for free. Check with Gumbo Limbo Nature Center (site #87) about guided field trips.

Directions: From intersection of US 1 and SR 794 (Yamato Rd.) in Boca Raton, drive south on US 1 appx. 0.5 mi., turn left (E) on NE 40th St.

(Spanish River Blvd.), drive 0.5 mi. to Ocean Blvd. and turn right (S); park entrance is 0.2 mi. on right (W).

Open Fri.-Mon. (call), 8 a.m. to sundown. (561) 393-7815 www.ci.boca-raton.fl.us/rec/parks/spanishriver.shtm

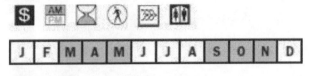

87 Gumbo Limbo Nature Center

This nature center has a boardwalk through tropical maritime hammock good for songbirds like waterthrushes on migration, continuing on to mangroves out to the Intracoastal Waterway (ICW); don't miss the observation tower! Check the ICW for plunging terns year-round and mergansers in winter, as well as the mangrove edge for waders like yellow-crowned night-herons. This site's real strength though is its comprehensive educational offerings; call ahead to join a guided tour or class on South Florida's unique habitats. Gumbo Limbo also offers off-site guided trips to places like Spanish River Park (site #86).

Directions: From intersection of US 1 and SR 794 (Yamato Rd.) in Boca Raton, drive south on US 1 appx. 0.5 mi., turn left (E) on NE 40th St. (Spanish River Blvd.), drive 0.5 mi. to Ocean Blvd. and turn right (S); park entrance is 1.2 mi. on right (W).

Open Mon.-Sat., 9 a.m. to 4 p.m.; Sun. noon to 4 p.m..
(561) 338-1473 www.gumbolimbo.org

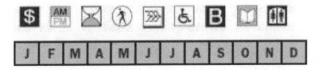

Map M
Night-Heron
Cluster

8 Fern Forest Nature
8 Center

This 244-acre natural area is a birder's delight with freshwater swamps, prairies and hardwood hammocks to explore. Part of the historical Cypress Creek Transverse glade, it is home to a whopping 34 species of fern, and shelters myriad birds. Painted buntings winter here and migrants like black-throated blue warblers and both waterthrushes migrate through. Check the prairie for wintering sparrows, and the tree line for raptors. An on-site nature center offers excellent programs and the boardwalk is wheelchair-accessible.

Directions: From intersection of US 441 and SR 814 (W. Atlantic Blvd.) in Margate, drive east on SR 814 appx. 1.2 mi. and turn right (S) on S. Lyons Rd.; entrance is on right. From I-95 take exit 36 (SR 814/W. Atlantic Blvd.) and drive 3.3 mi. west to S. Lyons. Stay in right lane, drive across Lyons/SW 46th Ave. and immediately turn right (N) to take loop south, which returns you to Lyons/46th Ave. Go 0.3 mi. south; entrance is on right (W).

Open Thurs.-Mon., 9 a.m. to 5 p.m.; 7 days/week in summer (call first). (954) 357-5198 www.broward.org/parks

J	F	M	A	M	J	J	A	S	O	N	D

8 9 Easterlin Park

This small urban park is comprised mostly of campsites and a disc golf course, but is surrounded by a stand of cypress and a thick hardwood hammock. Upon entering the park, turn right at the office and park at the end of the road, where the nature trail begins. Like many small urban refugia, this hammock is good for migrants like worm-eating warblers, cedar waxwings and yellow-billed cuckoos in migratory months.

Directions: From intersection of SR 811 (Dixie Hwy.) and SR 816 (Oakland Park Blvd.) in Oakland Park (N of Ft. Lauderdale), drive west appx. 1.4 mi. on SR 816 and turn right (N) on NW 9th Ave. (Powerline Rd.). After 0.4 mi., turn left (W) on NW 38th St. and drive 0.3 mi. to entrance on left (S).

Open Thurs.-Mon. (call first), 8 a.m. to 6 p.m. (winter); 8 a.m. to 7:30 p.m. (summer). (954) 357-5190 www.broward.org/parks

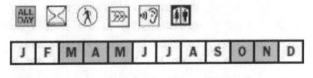

9 0 Hugh Taylor Birch State Park

This is a pleasant site to bird in cooler months and its 2-mile circular drive through the park allows easy pedestrian, wheelchair or vehicular access to some of the park's best birding. Watch the hammocks for songbird migrants like American redstarts, the mangrove edge for yellow-crowned night-herons, and the freshwater lagoons for anhingas and more. Canoes are available to explore the lagoon system. Two brief nature trails give more in-depth hammock experiences; also watch for magnificent frigatebird flyovers from the adjacent beaches.

Directions: From intersection of US 1 and SR 838 (E. Sunrise Blvd.), drive east on SR 838 appx. 1.0 mi. The park entrance is on the left (N).

Open year-round, 8 a.m. to sunset. (954) 564-4521
www.floridastateparks.org/hughtaylorbirch

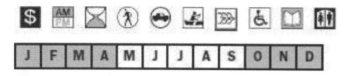

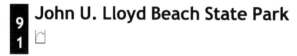

John U. Lloyd Beach State Park
91

Once overrun with invasive Australian pines, ongoing management is returning this park to its original, native condition. Check the beaches via the boardwalk accesses for wintering shorebirds like black-bellied plovers. The regenerating Barrier Island Nature Trail and the sea grape trees lining most of the parking lots are worth checking in migration for prairie warblers, ovenbirds and others. The jetty at the north end offers a tantalizing vantage for sea watching; keep an eye peeled for something interesting following the cruise ships as they return to the adjacent Port Everglades.

Directions: From intersection of US 1 and SR A1A in Dania (S of Ft. Lauderdale Int'l Airport), drive east on SR A1A (Dania Beach Blvd.) appx. 1.8 mi. to park entrance on right (N).

Open year-round, 8 a.m. to sunset. (954) 923-2833
www.floridastateparks.org/lloydbeach

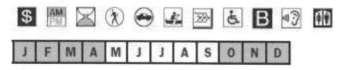

West Lake Park and Ann Kolb Nature Center
9

2

West Lake Park consists of the Anne Kolb Nature Center (N) and West Lake Park Recreation Area (S) located on Sheridan Street. West Lake has a north and south basin located west of the Intracoastal Waterway (ICW). Many short trails are available. At Ann Kolb, bird the mangrove boardwalks for yellow-crowned night-herons, and check the vantages of the ICW for shorebirds, gulls and terns. Look for soaring short-tailed hawks in winter. The nature center exhibit hall (open 9 a.m. to 5 p.m., call ahead) has a small entrance fee. Canoe/kayak rentals and boat tours of the mangroves are available. As in all of South Florida, even birding the trees in the parking lot can be fruitful; this turned up a vagrant thick-billed vireo from the Bahamas in May 2005. West Lake Park (S) has an entrance fee on weekends and holidays.

Directions: From intersection of US 1 and SR 822 (Sheridan St.) in Hollywood, drive east on SR 822 appx. 1.2 mi. West Lake Park is on right (S) side of road and the nature center is 100 yds. farther on the left (N) side.

Open Thurs.-Mon., 8 a.m. to 7:30 p.m., summer (call first); 8 a.m. to 6 p.m., fall to spring. (954) 357-5161 www.broward.org/parks

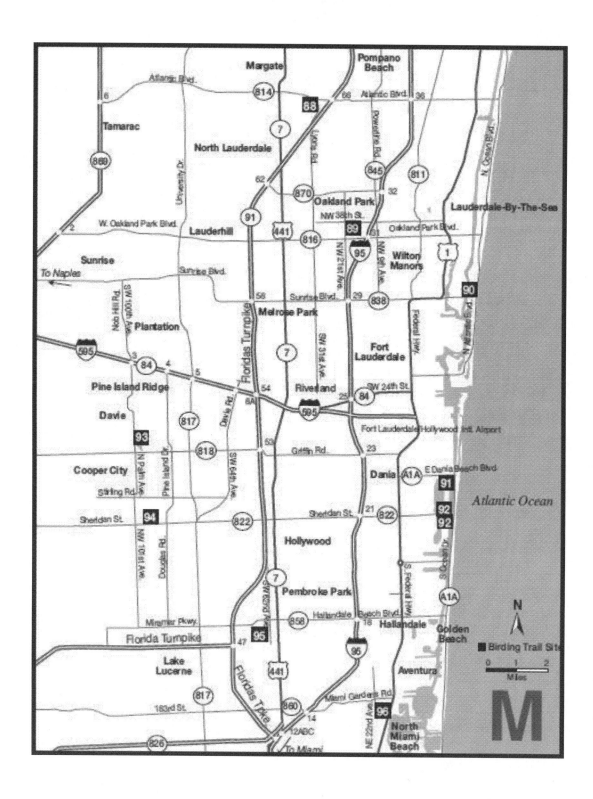

9 3 Tree Tops Park and Pine Island Ridge Natural Area

Tree Tops Park is the more developed of these two adjacent properties, with recreational fields, playgrounds, picnic shelters, restrooms and a visitor center. Nevertheless, its oaks can be worth checking for songbird migrants and its wetland boardwalk is reliable for purple gallinule all year, and occasional blue-winged teal, ring-necked and wood ducks in winter. Pine Island Ridge is accessed via a trail that begins behind the Tree Tops Visitor Center, and winds through towering oaks into the property. This narrow parcel has sandy, multi-use paths (shared with horses) that extend to more remote areas good for great horned and screech-owls. The thicker hammock to the left, after the trail splits, is a good location in migration. To the right, the trail continues on for quite a way, and the park gets progressively wider. Check the park website for a schedule of educational programs. Entrance fee on weekends and holidays only.

Directions: From intersection of SR 818 (Griffin Rd.) and Davie Rd. in Davie, drive west on SR 818 appx. 2.9 mi. and turn right (N) on SW 100th Ave. (Palm Ave.); entrance is appx. 0.5 mi. on right.

Open Thurs.-Mon. (call first), 8 a.m. to 6 p.m. (winter); 8 a.m. to 7:30 p.m. (summer). (954) 357-5130 www.broward.org/parks

9 4 Brian Piccolo Park

At first glance, this is an unlikely birding spot, with its assortment of baseball, football, soccer and cricket fields. Look a little closer though,

97

and you'll notice posts with flagging tape roping off holes in the middle of fields: this is one of the best sites to easily see Florida burrowing owls in the state. The owl population here is actually on the rise, and they're the pride and joy of park staff, who accommodate the birds' sometimes inconvenient choices of burrow locations. Respect their space, and you'll get excellent views. They even hunt on game nights, when insects are attracted to the ball fields' lights! Formerly, smooth-billed anis were sometimes found along the power line easement at the back of the park, but now, this is a single species site, and what a sight they are! Entrance fee applies only on weekends and holidays.

Directions: From intersection of US 441 and SR 822 (Sheridan St.), drive west on SR 822 appx. 4.0 mi.; park entrance is on right (N), just west of the intersection with Pine Island Rd.

Open all year, 8 a.m. to 7:30 p.m. (954) 357-5150
www.broward.org/parks

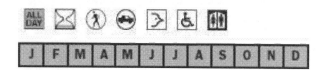

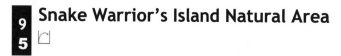

95 Snake Warrior's Island Natural Area

This 53-acre property is fully wheelchair-accessible and features paved trails winding between a series of wetlands. Acquired for its historical as well as its environmental value, this site hosts wintering blue-winged teal and ring-necked ducks, belted kingfishers, the full complement of South Florida wading birds, both yellowlegs and Wilson's snipe, as well as occasional nesting killdeer in summer.

Directions: From intersection of US 441 and SR 858 (Hallandale Beach Blvd.) in Miramar (west of Hollywood), drive 0.3 mi. west on SR 858 and turn left (S) on SW 62nd Ave; entrance is 0.5 mi. on right (W).

Open Thurs.-Mon., 9 a.m. to 5 p.m. (call first). (954) 357-5161
www.broward.org/parks

96 Greynolds Park

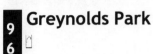

This park includes a golf course, multi-use trails and extensive mangrove boardwalks. Like many urban oases, Neotropical migrants are thick in the patches of tropical hardwood hammock, most easily accessed from the hammock trail at the parking area opposite the Nature Center. Black-throated blue warblers, redstarts and ovenbirds are all common visitors in April and October. Entrance fee on weekends and holidays only.

Directions: From intersection of US 1 and SR 860 (Miami Gardens Dr.) in North Miami Beach, drive west on SR 860 appx. 0.7 mi. and turn left (S) on NE 22nd Ave. The park entrance is on the left (E).

Open all year, sunrise to sunset. (305) 945-3425
www.miamidade.gov/parks

Map N
Cuckoo
Cluster

A. D. Barnes Park

7

This site is an oasis for migrant songbirds in urban Miami. Bypass the recreational fields/swimming pool and head to the nature center and woods on the park's north side. A paved path and wheelchair-accessible canopy platform wind through oak hammock, providing good views of songbirds like black-throated blue warblers and American redstarts in spring/fall. The nature center is open 9 to 5, closed Mon.-Tues.

Directions: From intersection of Palmetto Expressway and Bird Rd. (SW 40th St.) in West Miami, drive 0.5 mi. east on Bird Rd. and turn left (N) onto SW 72nd Ave. The park entrance is 0.2 mi. on the right (E).

Open Mon.-Fri., 8 a.m. to 5 p.m., Sat.-Sun. 9 a.m. to 5 p.m.
(305) 666-5883 www.miamidade.gov/parks

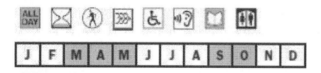

9 8 Crandon Park: Bear Cut Preserve and Beach

This park occupies the north end of Key Biscayne and spans both sides of Crandon Blvd. The preserve is at the northeast end, behind the Crandon Visitors and Nature Center, and includes a boardwalk through mangroves good for breeding mangrove cuckoos, prairie warblers and black-whiskered vireos. Coastal hammock trails have white-crowned pigeons and migrants like Cape May warblers. Gray kingbirds hawk for insects in open areas in spring/summer, and common ground-doves scratch in sandy spots along the trail. Look for ospreys, broad-winged hawks and falcons in fall along the sand dune trail. The beach is good for shorebirds, terns, gulls and plovers. Mudflats have piping plovers in winter.

Directions: From intersection of US 1 and SR 913 (Rickenbacker Toll Causeway), drive south on SR 913 appx. 4.5 mi. to entrance on left. Access the entrance drive via the second median crossover lane (North Beach Entrance) after the conspicuous information station on southbound SR 913.

Open 8 a.m. to dusk. (305) 365-3018 www.miamidade.gov/parks

99 Bill Baggs Cape Florida State Park

This site occupies the southern tip of Key Biscayne and is critical stopover habitat for migratory birds. In summer, gray kingbirds breed here and frigatebirds soar overhead. In winter, shorebirds like Wilson's plovers ply the beachfront. During migration, late March to May and again in September and October, the nature trails and even parking lot sea grape trees are alive with songbird migrants like Cape May and blackpoll warblers, and yellow-billed cuckoos. Beachgoers can be plentiful on weekends in sunny weather, but the nature trails are relatively untraveled.

Directions: From intersection of US 1 and SR 913 (Rickenbacker Toll Causeway) east of Coral Gables, drive south on SR 913 to park entrance at end of road.

Open all year, 8 a.m. to sunset. (305) 361-5811
www.floridastateparks.org/capeflorida

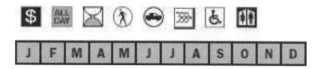

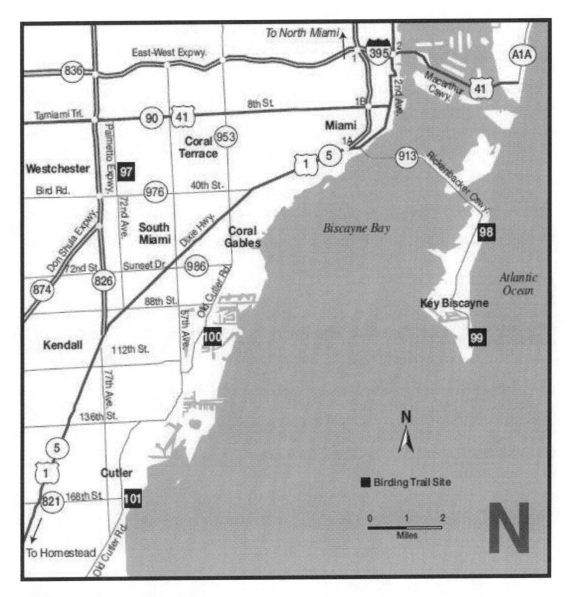

100 Matheson Hammock Park

This park can be thought of in three parts. The northernmost entrance offers two parking areas, the first of which is immediately after turning east off of Old Cutler. Here you can access the park-like portion of the property, comprised of grassy fields with tall hardwoods that occasionally host migratory songbirds and vagrants from the tropics. If you drive further east down the entrance road, you will be assessed an entrance fee in exchange for access to the water. The wading beach can be worth checking at low tide for waders and shorebirds; the swimming beach provides access for scoping Biscayne Bay for seabirds and wintering loons. Both can be busy with beachgoers in appropriate weather. Just south of the main entrance, on the opposite (W) side of Old Cutler Rd. is a parking lot pull-off for the hammock trails portion of the property. This is the most natural portion of the park and an access road from the south end of the parking lot makes birding for migrant songbirds easier.

Directions: From intersection of US 1 and SR 986 (Sunset Dr./SW 72nd St.) in South Miami, drive east on SR 986 appx. 1.7 mi. and turn right (S) on Old Cutler Rd.; parking area is 1.6 mi. on left (E).

Open all year, 7 a.m. to sunset. (305) 665-5475
www.miamidade.gov/parks

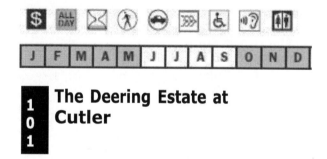

101 The Deering Estate at Cutler

This once-private historic estate, including its surrounding mangrove forests, towering tropical hardwoods and remnant pine rockland, is now a public park. You can freely bird the immediate area around the historic buildings and grounds for migratory songbirds, mangrove cuckoos and white-crowned pigeons. To see the rest of the more extensive property (and birds like black-whiskered vireo, limpkin and more), join one of the natural area tours included in your admission fee. For earlier access, check the website for monthly, early morning guided walks. Don't forget to check the boat basin for plovers, and the occasional endangered manatee or American crocodile!

Directions: From intersection of US 1 and SW 168th St. south of Kendall, drive 2.4 mi. east on SW 168th St. to park entrance on the right just before the end of the road.

Open daily except Christmas and Thanksgiving, 10 a.m. to 5 p.m. (305) 235-1668 × 242 www.deeringestate.org

Map O
Pine Rockland
Cluster

1 0 2 **Castellow Hammock Preserve**

This 112-acre park has a bird and butterfly garden that sports multicolored painted buntings in winter and migrants such as worm-eating warblers and American redstarts in spring and fall. Its hardwood hammock is a remnant of a once more widespread South Florida habitat and includes an invitingly shady trail great for songbirds. Approach the nature center slowly from the parking lot to avoid flushing birds in the garden; nature trail departs from the back side of the nature center. Nighttime owl prowls are scheduled in advance; call for more information.

Directions: From intersection of US 1 and Hainlin Mill Dr. (SW 216th St.) south of Cutler Ridge, drive west on Hainlin Mill Dr. 4.5 mi. and turn left (S) on Farm Life Rd. (SW 162nd Ave.); park entrance is 0.4 mi. on left (E).

Park open Wed.-Sun., 9 a.m. to 5 a.m. Birders are welcome to walk into the park from the gate before/after hours. (305) 242-7688
www.miamidade.gov/parks

103 Biscayne National Park: Convoy Point

This small mainland component of the larger National Park is the most easily accessed portion. On the drive in, listen carefully in the summer for mangrove cuckoos and black-whiskered vireos calling from the mangrove edge. At the parking area, walk the brief waterfront trail to the point, watching for winter/spring spotted sandpipers on the rocks, magnificent frigatebirds overhead and yellow-crowned night-herons skulking at the water's edge. Offshore keys included in the park can be excellent for migrant songbirds, but are accessible only by motorboat. January to April, Sunday tours are available to the keys, for a fee. Call (305) 230-1100 for details.

Directions: From intersection of US 1 and Lucy St. (SW 328th St.) in Homestead, drive east 7.5 mi. to park entrance at end of road.

Open 7 a.m. to 5:30 p.m. (305) 230-7275 www.nps.gov/bisc

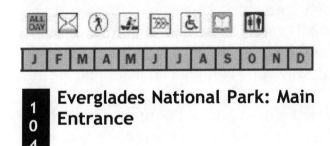

104 Everglades National Park: Main Entrance

The preeminent birding destination of South Florida, with many hotspots and some of the most abundant wading bird populations in the U.S. First, stop at the Ernest F. Coe Visitor Center for maps/checklists; check native plants here for hummingbirds. Next, stop at the Royal Palm Visitor Center, where two excellent trails begin. The Anhinga Trail is a photographer's paradise, with stunning views of herons (American bitterns on occasion) and purple gallinules. The Gumbo Limbo Trail passes through tropical hardwood hammock, where great crested (and sometimes brown-crested) flycatchers and warblers occur during winter and migration.

From fall to spring, the first mile of Old Ingraham Hwy. (near Royal Palm; ask staff for directions) can have limpkins, snail kites, mottled ducks, shorebirds and waders; look for least bitterns in spring/summer. Check Research Rd. for white-tailed kites. The Long Pine Key area offers bluebirds, brown-headed nuthatches, pine warblers, owls and woodpeckers. Along Main Park Rd., look overhead for soaring short-tailed hawks (dark morph is more common), American bitterns and wading birds. Mahogany Hammock's boardwalk is home to barred owls and wintering/migrating warblers. Sandhill cranes feed in the prairies.

Paurotis Pond often hosts a rookery (late winter-early summer) with wood storks, roseate spoonbills, herons and ibises. Whitecrowned pigeons (present all year; more common in summer) may be found at Nine-Mile Pond and along Main Park Rd. to Flamingo. At West Lake, check for waterfowl and for warblers along the boardwalk trail. Look for white-crowned pigeons and songbirds along the Snake Bight Trail, and waders and shorebirds from the boardwalk at trail's end (mosquitoes are abundant on this trail!). Patient birders may see mangrove cuckoos between the Snake Bight Trail and Flamingo; they become more vocal and easier to find in spring. Waterfowl and waders can be abundant at Mrazek Pond.

The Flamingo Visitor Center lies at the end of the road. Check the sightings list and wait for low tide, when pelicans, shorebirds, waders and black skimmers may be seen. In winter, check around Flamingo for scissor-tailed flycatchers and western kingbirds. On some winter mornings, Eco Pond hosts large numbers of wading birds, including spoonbills, wood storks and egrets. Look for shorebirds such as black-necked stilts in the pond during spring/summer. Canoeing to Snake Bight from Flamingo (2 to 6 miles round-trip, depending on your route) from fall to spring can yield large numbers of shorebirds, waders (such as spoonbills and reddish egrets) and white pelicans. Lesser black-backed gulls, bald eagles and peregrine falcons may also be present.

The area is best on a falling tide; ask at the Flamingo Visitor Center for directions and advice. Canoe/kayak rentals are available at Flamingo Marina.

Directions: From intersection of US 1 and SR 9336 in Florida City, drive 8.7 mi. west on SR 9336 to the main park entrance.

Open all year, 24 hours/day; Visitor Center open 9 a.m. to 5 p.m. (305) 242-7700 www.nps.gov/ever

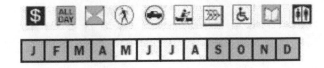

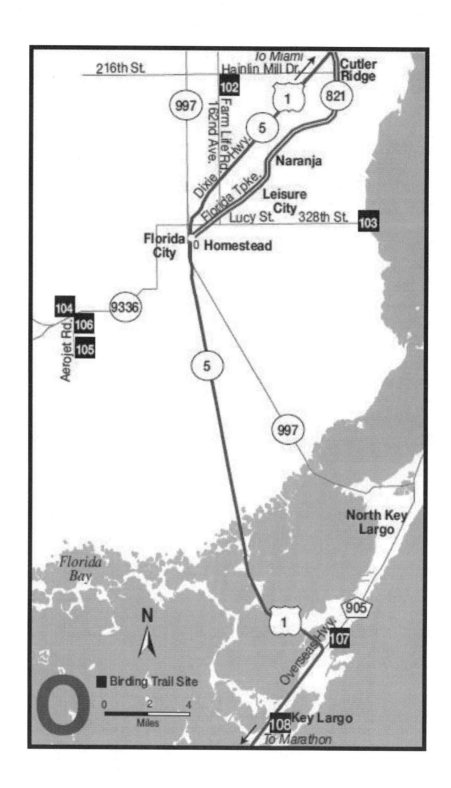

105 Southern Glades Wildlife and Environmental Area

This site is worth a quick stop as you are on your way to other sites in the area. Predominately marsh and marl prairie with a sprinkling of tree islands, this property provides habitat for a plethora of sparrows and blackbirds along the roadside, as well as wading birds typical of Everglades marshes. Watch skyward for soaring short-tailed hawks and swallow-tailed kites. Check the brushy areas near the abandoned missile complex at the southern end of the road for white-crowned pigeons (a very northern population). Visit before first light and listen closely – a small, remnant population of Cape Sable seaside sparrows occurs here.

Directions: From intersection of US 1 and SR 9336 in Florida City, drive 8.1 mi. west on SR 9336 and turn left (S) on Aerojet Rd. (at the "Everglades Youth Camp" sign); the site is 0.8 mi. ahead.

Open all year, dawn to dusk. (954) 746-1789, (561) 686-8800 ext. 6635
MyFWC.com/viewing/recreation/wmas or www.sfwmd.gov

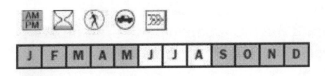

| J | F | M | A | M | J | J | A | S | O | N | D |

106 Frog Pond Area ("Lucky Hammock")

You may not believe this site when you first drive up to it. Although the actual site encompasses a large stretch of land around it, the main birding spot is a small tropical hammock that covers only a quarter of an acre. Don't be fooled – this hotspot is known to local birders and is a stop on any day-long birding tour of the county. An island of lush growth in the middle of agricultural fields, Lucky Hammock is a haven for resident warblers, vireos, cuckoos, flycatchers and buntings (both indigo and painted). Catch it early in the morning during migration and you may be treated to a virtual rainfall of birds. This site is also known to attract rarities such as sulphur-bellied flycatcher.

Directions: From intersection of US 1 and SR 9336 in Florida City, drive 8.1 mi. west on SR 9336 and turn left (S) on Aerojet Rd. (at the "Everglades Youth Camp" sign); the site is 0.3 mi. on the right.

Open all year, dawn to dusk. (561) 686-8800 ext. 6635
www.sfwmd.gov

Dagny Johnson Key Largo Hammock Botanical State Park

This park's 2,500 acres encompass the largest remaining tracts of rockland hammock in the continental U.S. A 0.75-mile paved walking/biking trail takes you into the main public part of the habitat, where you can find breeding populations of black-whiskered vireos, mangrove cuckoos and white-crowned pigeons; warblers drip from the trees during migration. An additional 4 miles of paved trails, as well as off-trail possibilities, are accessible after obtaining a free backcountry permit (at neighboring John D. Pennekamp State Park). This beautiful park suffers only from lack of birder use. Rarities such as La Sagra's flycatcher, thick-billed vireo and Zenaida dove have been found here in the past; it is only a matter of time before the birding public documents these and other rarities again!

Directions: From intersection of US 1 and CR 905 in Key Largo, drive 0.4 mi. north on CR 905 to the main entrance on the right (E).

Open all year, 8 a.m. to sunset. (305) 451-1202
www.floridastateparks.org/keylargohammock

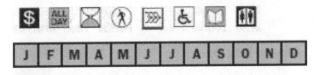

John Pennekamp Coral Reef State Park

While much of the property lies underwater, this park contains 2,900 acres of magnificent mangrove swamps, hardwood hammocks, rivers, springs and coastal rocky areas. Birders will find three short walking trails and the coastal areas of interest for the variety of species they offer, including gray kingbirds, short-tailed hawks and such Keys specialties as mangrove cuckoo, black-whiskered vireo and white-crowned pigeon. Walk or bike around the park, or put in a canoe from the boat launch for a different type of birding experience. Glass bottom boat tours of the reef can be good for pelagic species such as gannets, petrels and sooty terns. Be sure to ask about recent sightings at the visitor center, because this park has a propensity for attracting tropical vagrants, including Bahama mockingbird and thick-billed vireo.

Directions: From intersection of US 1 and CR 905 in Key Largo, drive 3.7 mi. south on US 1 to entrance (mile marker 102.5) on left (E).

Open all year, 8 a.m. to sunset. (305) 451-1202
www.floridastateparks.org/pennekamp

Map P
White-Crowned Pigeon
Cluster

Long Key State
9 **Park**

Mangrove swamp, mudflats, rockland hammock, beach and coastal berm are some of the habitats that attract a variety of species to this site. Roseate spoonbills and reddish egrets (among others) can be seen along the shoreline at low tide. The 1.25-mile Golden Orb Trail takes you past mudflats hosting shorebirds like ruddy turnstones and through tidal swamps where warblers and vireos spend the heat of the day and mangrove cuckoos call. Hammocks provide foraging areas for white-crowned pigeons, and even the parking lot edges with their sea grapes have proven productive, yielding a western spindalis in 2005.

Directions: Entrance on US 1 north of Marathon at mile marker 67.5, ocean side.

Open all year, 8 a.m. to sunset. (305) 664-4815
www.floridastateparks.org/longkey

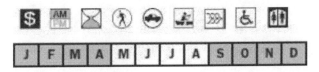

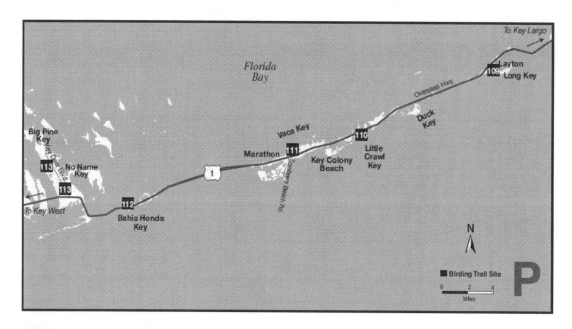

110 Curry Hammock State Park

This coastal park offers rockland hammock and beach viewing of waders and shorebirds, much like other sites in the Keys. However, of particular interest to birders is the yearly hawk watch conducted here. Between mid-September and early November and you can join in the official raptor count for the Keys! Rangers and volunteers offer educational contacts for visitors, while counting off the thousands of buteos, accipiters, falcons and eagles that pass by the viewing area each fall. This site offers a one-of-a-kind experience during this particular season. A nature trail on the bay side takes visitors through a tropical hardwood hammock. An excellent site for white-crowned pigeons and kayaking.

Directions: Entrance on US 1 north of Marathon at mile marker 56, ocean (E) side.

Open all year, 8 a.m. to sunset. (305) 289-2690

www.floridastateparks.org/curryhammock

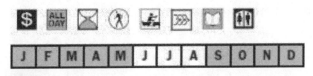

Crane Point Museum and Nature Center

1
1
1

This 63-acre site is a tropical oasis amidst the development in the middle Keys. Thatch palm and tropical hardwood hammock, along with occasional freshwater ponds, provide habitat for both resident and migrating warblers, vireos, tanagers and thrushes. White-crowned pigeons can be found in the canopies looking for poisonwood berries. A trail loop system with educational signage takes you through four hammock types. Tidal lagoons, as well as the tip of the peninsula looking out at Rachel Key in Florida Bay, give views of spring-nesting seabirds and year-round views of waders. Shorebirds congregate at low tide and magnificent frigatebirds wheel among the brown pelicans overhead. Watch the mangroves here for (you guessed it!) mangrove cuckoos.

Directions: Entrance on US 1 in Marathon at mile marker 50 (Sombrero Beach Rd. intersection).

Open all year, 9 a.m. to 5 p.m. Mon.-Sat.; noon to 5 p.m. Sun. (305) 743-9100 www.cranepoint.net

Bahia Honda State Park

1
1

2

This site offers the best of Keys birding habitats: tropical hardwood hammock, coastal berm and beach/dune communities. Walk the two short nature trails at either end of the park, and drive or bike the roadway slowly watching the sea grape and poisonwood trees for white-crowned pigeons and warblers feeding on the fruits. Low tide along the beach offers shorebirds and waders in the wrackline. Take the trail up onto the decommissioned bridge for a gull's-eye view of the bay and ocean; hawk watching here is good in fall. Look for songbirds during spring migration.

Directions: Entrance on US 1 south of Marathon at mile marker 37, ocean (E) side.

Open all year, 8 a.m. to sunset. (305) 872-2353
www.floridastateparks.org/bahiahonda

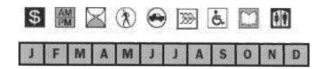

National Key Deer Refuge: Blue Hole, Jack Watson and Fred Mannillo Trails

These short trails are complimentary in their exposure of different habitats within the refuge. Blue Hole Trail is 0.25 miles long and partially circles one of the few bodies of fresh water on Big Pine Key, a feature that not only attracts green herons and belted kingfishers, but also brings in migrating warblers, vireos and thrushes. Jack Watson Trail passes 0.6 miles through pine rockland, an uncommon habitat this far south, and brings you close to the island's woodpeckers and resident warblers as well as species like gray kingbirds and white-crowned pigeons. Be sure to check out the ADA-showcase Mannillo Trail that ends with a viewing platform over a wetland. Key deer and Antillean nighthawks are extra treats.

Directions: From mile marker 30.5 on US 1 on Big Pine Key, turn north on Key Deer Blvd. and drive 2.8 mi. to Blue Hole parking on left; Jack Watson trail is 0.3 mi. farther north on Key Deer Blvd., also on left. Visitor center is located in the Big Pine Key shopping mall on Key Deer Blvd. 1/8 mi. north of the intersection of US 1 and Key Deer Blvd.

Open all year, sunrise to sunset. (305) 872-2239
www.fws.gov/nationalkeydeer/

Map Q
Key West and Tortugas Cluster

1 1 4 Key West Tropical Forest and Botanical Garden

This 15-acre site offers one of the richest birding experiences in the lower Keys, with 160+ species recorded. Containing tropical hardwood hammock and the only freshwater ponds on Key West and Stock Island, this property is a magnet for resident species such as white-crowned pigeons and black-whiskered vireos. Check the large trees at the entrance for eastern and western kingbirds and scissor-tailed flycatchers – sometimes all in the same tree! Migrations bring fallouts of tanagers, thrushes, buntings and flycatchers, as well as sharp-shinned and broad-winged hawks overhead. Ask about recent sightings of rarities, as this oasis is known to attract species including Bahama mockingbird. Special birders' hours offered in April; please call ahead. New habitat and trail improvements have been made. Donations are appreciated.

Directions: From mile marker 4.5 on US 1 north of Key West, turn north onto College Rd. and drive 0.1 mi. to the site entrance on the right.

Open all year, 10 a.m. to 4 p.m. or anytime by request.
(305) 296-1504 www.kwbgs.org, www.keywestbotanicalgarden.org

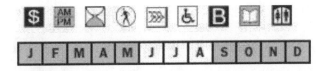

1 1 5 Fort Zachary Taylor Historic State Park

This park is the first dry land that many migrants see on their northward journey, and the last opportunity to fuel up when heading south. Thus, this small site hosts concentrations of birds at certain times of year. Spring warblers provide color and lessons in song identification, and fall brings southbound raptors. Year-round, this site has hundreds of frigatebirds, shorebirds and seabirds that congregate on the seawall and breakwaters. Vagrants and rarities occur here frequently, including Antillean short-eared owl, western spindalis, red-legged honeycreeper and loggerhead kingbird.

Directions: On US 1 in Key West, drive south to mile marker 0.5 (stay on US 1 when it turns to the right and becomes Whitehead St.) and turn left on Southard St; entrance is 0.2 mi. on left.

Open all year, 8 a.m. to sunset. (305) 292-6713
www.floridastateparks.org/forttaylor

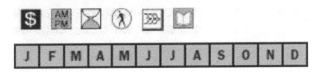

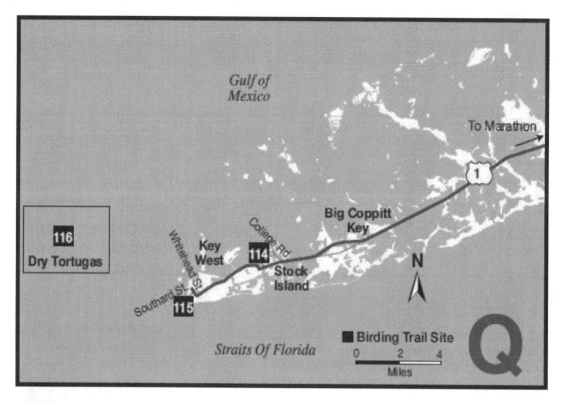

Map labels: Gulf of Mexico · To Marathon · 1 · Big Coppitt Key · 116 Dry Tortugas · College Rd · Key West · 114 · Whitehead St · Southard St · Stock Island · 115 · N · Straits Of Florida · ■ Birding Trail Site · 0 2 4 Miles · Q

1 1 6 Dry Tortugas National Park

Avid birders know the incredible possibilities that exist on this remote island oasis. The southernmost point in the continental U.S., this park offers the seagoing birder opportunities to view species that occur nowhere else in the country. Bush Key hosts the only significant breeding colony of sooty terns in the U.S., and from February through August there are literally tens of thousands of these birds loudly claiming their territories. Intermixed with the "sooties", brown noddies also nest here, and the occasional black noddy can be found by carefully picking through the birds perched on the coaling docks. Brown boobies perch on the pilings with the occasional roseate tern, masked boobies nest on nearby Hospital Key, and vagrant red-footed boobies are seen almost every year. Pelagic species such as bridled terns, Audubon's shearwaters and band-rumped storm-petrels are seen in the channels. Migratory fallouts during late April and early May can be the stuff of legend, with exhausted trans-Gulf migrants settling on the first dry land they have come across in thousands of miles; it is not uncommon to experience 25-warbler mornings after the right weather conditions the night before. In recent years, an Antillean short-eared owl has regularly been spotted at the main Fort. Common birds in the Tortugas include magnificent frigatebirds, peregrine falcons and shorebirds such as ruddy turnstones. This is truly a special birding destination.

Directions: The park is a 2.5 hour boat trip off of mainland Florida's southwest coast. Commercial ferries and seaplanes leave from Key West; call park headquarters for contact information.

Open all year. (305) 242-7700 www.nps.gov/drto

Help Us Maintain the Trail!

The Great Florida Birding and Wildlife Trail's mission is to conserve and enhance Florida's wildlife habitat by promoting birding and wildlife viewing activities, conservation education and economic opportunity. Help the FWC maintain the Trail by "adopting" sites in your area. For example, if you find an error in the guide or you see a Birding Trail road sign that needs repair, please let us know. As of May 2011, road signs have been completed in the East, West and Panhandle trail sections. Signs for the South section will be completed in 2011.

Your support and opinions are important to us. Have a site update or a comment about the Trail? Contact the Birding and Wildlife Trail coordinator at GFBT@MyFWC.com. Thanks!

Birder and wildlife viewer I.D.
Mail-in response form

Name_____

Street_____

City_____

State_____County_____

Zip_____Country_____

E-mail_____

Home phone_____

Work phone_____

Request for information

_____Add my name to your mailing list

_____Send mailings electronically

_____Send a bird checklist – also available online*

_____Send a Birding and Wildlife Trail sponsorship packet

_____Send a Birding and Wildlife Trail brochure

_____Send a Birding and Wildlife Trail Guide – also available online*

East_____West_____South_____Panhandle_____Send
"Birdwatching Basics" – also available online*

Other_____

_____

*www.floridabirdingtrail.com

The Great Florida Birding and Wildlife Trail is a program of the Florida Fish and Wildlife Conservation Commission.

MyFWC.com

Rate the Trail!
Mail-in response form

Your country, state and county of origin_____

_____

Where did you hear about the Trail?_____

_____

What is your goal in using the Trail? (e.g. finding a specific species of bird, seeing a diversity of birds and wildlife or simply enjoying the outdoors)._____

_____

_____

How long have you had this guide?_____

How many sites have you visited?_____

Which site was the best? Why?_____

_____

Which site was worst? Why?_____

_____

How many days have you spent birding or wildlife viewing in the last month? _____

How long was your last trip on the Birding and Wildlife Trail?

_____

How much money did you spend on lodging, food and gas on the above trip? $_____

Will you recommend the Trail to friends?_____

Please detach and mail us your valued response to the GFBWT address on page 39. **Thank you!**

Wings Over Florida Program

Wings Over Florida is a FREE award program open to all birders. Its purpose is to encourage you to identify as many Florida native birds as you can. As your skills improve and your bird list grows, you can apply for increasing levels of achievement. Full color certificates are awarded at five levels starting at 50 species (Beginner) and ending at 350 species (Elite Florida Birder). Simply fill out an FWC bird checklist and application sheet and send it to FWC to review. For an application and free bird checklist, contact:

Wings Over Florida Program
P.O. Box 6181
Tallahassee, FL 32314-6181

WOF@MyFWC.com
www.floridabirdingtrail.com

Birding and wildlife viewing ethics

Don't you hate it when the doorbell or telephone rings just as you settle down to dinner or a nap? While mere nuisances to us, disruptions in feeding and nesting routines can spell disaster for birds and wildlife, especially the cumulative effect of frequent disruptions, a common occurrence at busy sites. When a nesting bird is forced to fly, it may leave eggs or young exposed to temperature extremes or predators. A migratory bird may be exhausted and hungry from a long flight – it needs to rest and eat. With care and common sense, we can help protect the wildlife we love to watch. Consider these points:

- Stay back from concentrations of nesting or loafing waterbirds – a spotting scope may be a better choice than binoculars.

- Walk around groups of birds on the beach rather than forcing them to fly.

- Sit or crouch so that you appear smaller.

- Keep movements slow and steady rather than fast or sporadic.

- If viewing from your car, stay inside as long as possible. It acts as a viewing "blind" and the birds are less likely to fly if they don't recognize you as human.

- Stay on roads, trails and paths to minimize habitat disturbance.

- Do you occasionally use recordings to attract birds? If so, remember not to overuse them, or to try to attract rare or protected species.

Birding and wildlife viewing resources

There are many more resources for birding and wildlife viewing in Florida. Before your trip, check the Internet for area rare bird alert hotlines and statewide birding listservs to get an idea of what's being seen. If you're staying in an area for a longer visit, check local book and nature stores for area guides to birding published by local Audubon chapters or birders. The Great Florida Birding and Wildlife Trail guides are just a taste of the information available to plan your ultimate Florida vacation.

For more information

Or to be added to the mailing list for the Birding and Wildlife Trail's newsletter, *Kite Tales*, fill in the response form (including your name and address) on the previous page and mail to:

Great Florida Birding and Wildlife Trail (GFBWT)

620 South Meridian St.
Tallahassee, FL 32399-1600

or visit the Birding and Wildlife Trail's website at:
www.floridabirdingtrail.com

The *Kite Tales* newsletter includes news about the Trail and Trail-related events across the state. Information is also available regarding Trail sponsorship, site nominations for upcoming Trail sections, tips for better birding and the economic impact of this flourishing pastime. Take part in the continued development of this great resource for birders and wildlife watchers of all skill levels, while enjoying and ensuring continued concern for the conservation of Florida's fabulous avian and wildlife treasures!

Birders and wildlife viewers – flex your economic muscles!

Florida communities have long made land use choices to attract traditional tourists and their dollars. Birding is big business in Florida, too... but communities will only recognize that if we're visible. Your visibility and economic impact can encourage wildlife conservation. Some ways you can make youreself more visible:

- Wear bird and wildlife t-shirts.

- Take your binoculars into the restaurant with you.

- Ask local residents in restaurants, hotels, gas stations, etc. about where good birding and wildlife viewing locations might be in their area.

- Leave birder calling cards whenever you spend money, helping vendors make the connection between healthy wild lands and healthy economies (cards may be downloaded from www.floridabirdingtrail.com).

■ Put a birding bumper sticker or window decal on your car or business. It speaks for itself, so you don't have to.

Conserve wildlife by watching wildlife! It's more than a hobby...it's a legacy.

For the Birds!

The Great Florida Birding and Wildlife Trail helps everyone enjoy and conserve Florida's wildlife and wildlife habitats. A donation to the Wildlife Foundation of Florida helps us expand and enhance the Great Florida Birding and Wildlife Trail experience. With your support, we can continue to protect Florida's natural resources for future generations to enjoy.

If you would like to make a donation, please mail your check to:

Wildlife Foundation of Florida
Attn: GFBWT
P.O. Box 6181
Tallahassee, Florida 32314-6181

Note: Please write GFBWT in the memo section of your check. Thanks!

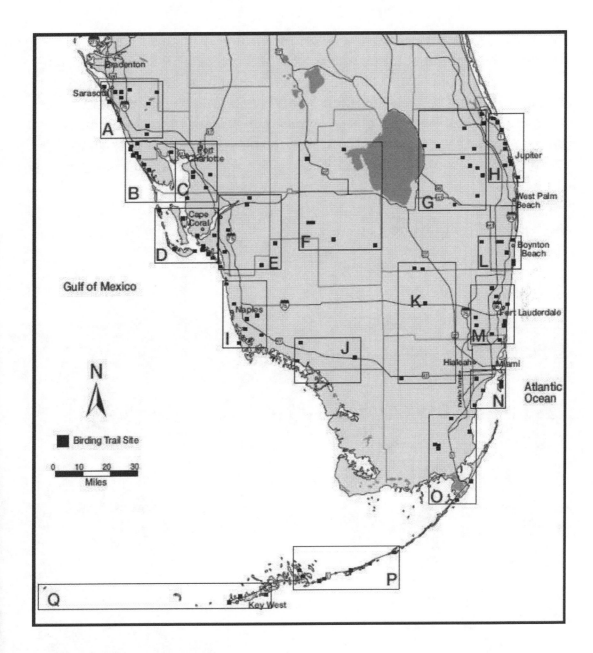

How to use this guide

We hope this guide will help you quickly and easily identify South
section birding and wildlife viewing sites of interest to you. Sites have

met criteria ensuring they are good for birding, and are able to withstand birder use. Maps show "clusters" of 1 to 10 sites within an hour's drive of one another. The map on the right shows the locations of these clusters; the letter in each box corresponds to the map for that cluster. Descriptions and directions for sites accompany each cluster map. You may want to use the maps in this guide along with a more detailed map book, such as a DeLorme *Florida Atlas and Gazetteer.*

Map Key
(see page 2 for City Locator)

A Myakka River Cluster

B Sandpiper Cluster

C Charlotte Harbor Cluster

D Piping Plover Cluster

E Wood Stork Cluster

F Short-tailed Hawk Cluster

G Okeechobee Cluster

H Spoonbill Cluster

I Mangrove Cluster

J Cypress Cluster

K Snail Kite Cluster

L Whistling-Duck Cluster

M Night-Heron Cluster

N Cuckoo Cluster

O Pine Rockland Cluster

P White-Crowned Pigeon Cluster

Made in United States
Orlando, FL
22 December 2024

56442044R00083